PRINCE

A LIFE IN PURPLE

(A BIOGRAPHY)

WRITTEN BY:

ELEANOR RIGGS

TABLE OF CONTENTS

INTRODUCTION

Prince Rogers Nelson, born on June 7, 1958, and tragically departed from this world on April 21, 2016, was an exceptional American artist. His multifaceted talents spanned the realms of singing, songwriting, musicianship, record production, and acting. Among the constellation of accolades and nominations that graced his career, he shines as one of the most brilliant luminaries of his musical generation.

Prince was an artist who defied convention and expectations. His image was a symphony of flamboyance and androgyny, an extraordinary fusion that left an indelible mark on pop culture. He didn't just sing; he painted with his voice. His vocal range was a kaleidoscope of emotions, spanning from the ethereal heights of his far-reaching falsetto to the electrifying intensity of his high-pitched screams.

But Prince's genius didn't stop with his vocal prowess; he was a virtuoso multi-instrumentalist. In the studio, he often played the roles of an entire band, demonstrating his mastery of a multitude of instruments. His ability to weave intricate melodies and rhythms, sculpting them into cohesive musical tapestries, was nothing short of mesmerizing.

Prince's music was a rich tapestry, interwoven with diverse genres. His compositions traversed the sonic landscapes of funk, R&B, rock, new wave, soul, synth-pop, pop, jazz, blues, and even ventured into the realms of hip-hop. Each note, each lyric, was a vibrant stroke on the canvas of his creativity. His music defied categorization, for it was a genre unto itself - the unique and ever-evolving sound of Prince.

What's even more remarkable is that Prince was not just the face and voice of his music; he was the mastermind behind every aspect of his artistry. He took the reins of his albums, steering them in directions that were groundbreaking. In doing so, he pioneered what is known as the "Minneapolis sound," a distinctive sonic tapestry that would leave an indelible mark on the music world.

In the symphony of American music, Prince was a virtuoso, a maestro who pushed the boundaries, shattered norms, and left an enduring legacy. His music, his style, and his spirit continue to inspire and resonate, reminding us that the power of artistic expression knows no bounds.

Hailing from the vibrant city of Minneapolis, Prince embarked on his legendary musical journey at a tender age, signing a record deal with Warner Bros. Records when he was just 19. With youthful exuberance, he unveiled his early creations in the form of "For You" in 1978 and "Prince" in 1979. These were the humble seeds of his phenomenal career.

However, it was in the early 1980s that Prince's star truly began to ascend. With "Dirty Mind" (1980), "Controversy" (1981), and "1999" (1982), he carved a path to critical acclaim, creating a sound that transcended genres and defined a generation. But it was his sixth album, "Purple Rain" (1984), that catapulted him into the stratosphere of stardom. Accompanied by his talented backing band, the Revolution, "Purple Rain" not only conquered the charts but also graced the silver screen in a movie of the same name, in which Prince himself starred. This was a milestone that etched his name in the annals of music history, with "Purple Rain" reigning supreme atop the Billboard 200 chart for a remarkable six consecutive months. The movie's soundtrack also earned Prince the prestigious Academy Award for Best Original Song Score.

Following this meteoric success, Prince evolved, and so did his artistic identity. He disbanded the Revolution but went on to release "Sign o' the Times" (1987), a masterpiece lauded by critics as the zenith of his career.

In 1993, ensnared in a contractual dispute with Warner Bros., Prince embarked on a peculiar and bold journey. He transformed his name into a symbol, a fusion of a hollow circle above a downward arrow crossed with a curlicues horn-shaped symbol and a short bar, often referred to as the "Love Symbol." Fans affectionately dubbed him The Artist Formerly Known as Prince (TAFKAP) or simply The Artist. His ingenuity knew no bounds, and this symbol became an emblem of his artistry.

In 1998, Prince found a new stage at Arista Records, and by 2000, he had reclaimed his original name. Over the next decade, he continued to captivate the world, with six of his albums storming the U.S. top 10 charts.

But the world lost this prodigious talent in April 2016. At the age of 57, Prince tragically succumbed to an accidental fentanyl overdose at his Paisley Park home and recording studio in Chanhassen, Minnesota. He left behind a musical treasure trove, with 39 released albums in his lifetime and a vault brimming with unreleased material, including fully completed albums and over 50 finished music videos. His posthumous works, "Piano and a Microphone 1983" (2018) and "Originals" (2019), continued to receive critical acclaim, a testament to his enduring influence.

Prince's impact extended far beyond his music sales. He stands among the best-selling music artists of all time, with over 100 million records sold worldwide. His accolades were as numerous as his notes, including the Grammy President's Merit Award, the American Music Awards for Achievement and of Merit, the Billboard Icon Award, an Academy Award, and a Golden Globe Award. His enduring legacy was further cemented by his induction into the Rock and Roll Hall of Fame in 2004, the UK Music Hall of Fame in 2006, and the Rhythm and Blues Music Hall of Fame in 2016. In 2022, he was posthumously honored twice with induction into the Black Music & Entertainment Walk of Fame.

The sheer volume of songs attributed to Prince is astounding, with estimates ranging from 500 to well over 1,000. Many of his compositions found new life through other artists' interpretations, such as "Nothing Compares 2 U," famously covered by Sinéad O'Connor, and "Manic Monday," brought to life by the Bangles. Prince's influence rippled across generations and continues to shape the musical landscape to this day.

ROOTS AND FORMATIVE YEARS

Prince's journey commenced in the heart of Minneapolis, where he was welcomed into the world on June 7, 1958. His origins bore the unmistakable imprint of music, with a jazz singer for a mother, Mattie Della (née Shaw), and a father, John Lewis Nelson, who was a pianist and a skilled songwriter. The roots of his family tree reached deep into the fertile soil of Louisiana, as all four of his grandparents hailed from that vibrant, culturally rich state.

Prince's lineage also boasted a fascinating connection to the esteemed black nationalist Mittie Maude Lena Gordon, his grand-aunt. She was a trailblazer in her own right, founding the Peace Movement of Ethiopia and championing the cause of emigration to West Africa as a response to the scourge of American white supremacy.

His family's musical legacy extended even further. The illustrious jazz drummer, Louis Hayes, held the distinction of being Prince's paternal cousin. The rhythms and melodies of their shared heritage surely resonated through their lives.

Prince's name itself bore the weight of tradition. He was christened "Prince" in homage to his father's most prominent stage name, "Prince Rogers," which his father used while performing alongside Prince's mother in the jazz ensemble, the Prince Rogers Trio. It was a moniker born from artistic collaboration, and in 1991, Prince's father shared a heartfelt reason for this choice. He expressed a desire for his son to fulfill all the aspirations he once harbored.

Yet, Prince harbored his own sentiments about his name. He preferred to be called "Skipper," a name that clung to him through the tapestry of his childhood. The artist known the world over as Prince once confided that he was "born epileptic" and that he grappled with seizures during his formative years. In a touching recollection, he recounted a pivotal moment when he informed his mother that he would no longer be afflicted. He simply told her, "Mom, I'm not going to be sick anymore," explaining that an angel had conveyed this message to him.

The Prince of Minneapolis shared his early years with a younger sister, Tyka, born on May 18, 1960. Music coursed through their veins, nurtured by their father's encouragement. Their upbringing was rooted in the Seventh-day Adventist Church, an evangelical denomination that instilled spiritual values alongside their musical gifts.

A captivating glimpse into the young Prince's life emerged in 2022 during a Minneapolis teachers' strike. WCCO-TV, while researching a previous teachers' strike in 1970, stumbled upon an interview with a pre-fame Prince. At the tender age of 11 or 12, he offered his perspective on the strike, stating, "I think they should get a better education too cause, um, and I think they should get some more money cause they work, they are working extra hours for us and all that stuff." In a poignant twist of history, this interview, where he didn't explicitly identify himself, was confirmed as his words through the diligent efforts of a Minneapolis historian and a former classmate who was part of Prince's first band. It stands as a rare and cherished relic from a formative chapter in the life of an icon.

The seeds of Prince's remarkable musical journey were sown at a tender age, as he composed his very first song, "Funk Machine," on his father's piano when he was just seven years old. This early creative spark foreshadowed the genius that would later captivate the world.

However, Prince's childhood was marked by the disintegration of his parents' marriage when he was ten years old. His mother, Mattie, found new love with Hayward Baker and together they welcomed a son named Omarr. This new familial constellation, unfortunately, led to a tumultuous relationship between Prince and Omarr, prompting Prince to frequently shuttle between his parents' homes, sometimes residing with his father and at other times with his mother and stepfather.

It was Hayward Baker, in a twist of fate, who introduced Prince to the electrifying world of live music, taking him to see the legendary James Brown in concert. This experience left an indelible mark on the young artist and, in an unforeseen turn of events, significantly bolstered the family's financial situation.

After a brief period living with his father, who gifted him his first guitar, Prince found himself in the basement of the Anderson family, their neighbors. His father had cast him out, and it was there, in that basement, that Prince's journey to musical greatness took a significant turn. It was in the Andersons' home that he befriended their son, Andre, who would later become known as André Cymone. This friendship would shape not only Prince's life but the musical landscape as well, as they embarked on a collaborative journey that would reverberate through the ages.

Prince's educational path wove through Minneapolis, from Bryant Junior High to Central High School. In high school, his interests extended beyond music, as he was a multi-sport athlete, participating in football, basketball, and baseball.

He even played on the junior varsity basketball team at Central. Even as an adult, the love of basketball remained a constant in his life, providing a balance to his musical pursuits.

Yet, his artistic spirit was not confined to sports alone. During his time at Bryant, he underwent formal training in classical ballet at the Minnesota Dance Theatre, an experience facilitated by the Urban Arts Program of Minneapolis Public Schools. This early exposure to the world of dance left a lasting impression on Prince, turning him into a steadfast advocate for dancers and their artistry. His commitment to the art form extended to saving the struggling Joffrey Ballet in Chicago during the 1990s through his financial support.

The web of destiny continued to spin as he crossed paths with songwriter and producer Jimmy Jam in 1973. Jam was profoundly impressed by Prince's innate musical talent, his mastery of a wide array of instruments, and his tireless work ethic. This encounter would prove pivotal, paving the way for Prince to ascend to the heights of musical greatness.

CAREER

EMERGING AS A MUSICAL FORCE (1975–1984)

The genesis of Prince's extraordinary career can be traced back to 1975 when Pepe Willie, the husband of Prince's cousin Shauntel, embarked on a musical journey. He formed the band 94 East, enlisting the talents of Marcy Ingvoldstad and Kristie Lazenberry. To bolster their sound, they brought in the budding talents of André Cymone and the young Prince. In this collaborative venture, Willie was the songwriter, while Prince lent his guitar prowess. Together, Prince and Willie co-wrote the track "Just Another Sucker." Their musical collaboration led to the recording of tracks that would later become the album "Minneapolis Genius – The Historic 1977 Recordings."

In 1976, shortly after graduating from Central High School, Prince took a significant step in his musical journey. Teaming up with producer Chris Moon, he ventured into Moon's Minneapolis studio to create a demo tape. This was a pivotal moment, as this demo tape, brimming with Prince's raw talent, was the key that would unlock the doors of the music industry.

With the demo tape in hand, but unable to secure a recording contract, Moon turned to Owen Husney, a Minneapolis businessman with a keen eye for talent. Husney was not only impressed by Prince's musical gifts but also saw the potential for something truly special. He signed the 19-year-old Prince to a management contract and played a pivotal role in shaping his early career.

Together, they created a new demo at Sound 80 Studios in Minneapolis, with the assistance of producer/engineer David Z. This demo, accompanied by a press kit produced at Husney's ad agency, garnered interest from several major record companies, including the likes of Warner Bros. Records, A&M Records, and Columbia Records.

In a momentous turn of events, Prince secured a recording contract with Warner Bros. Records. The record label, recognizing his immense talent, agreed to a deal that would grant Prince creative control for three albums while allowing him to retain his publishing rights. With this arrangement in place, Prince and Husney left Minneapolis, setting their sights on Sausalito, California.

It was in Sausalito that Prince's inaugural album, "For You," took shape. Recorded at Record Plant Studios and later mixed in Los Angeles, the album saw its release on April 7, 1978. A testament to Prince's extraordinary abilities, the album notes revealed that he had written, produced, arranged, composed, and played all 27 instruments on the recording, with the exception of the song "Soft and Wet," which featured lyrics co-written by Chris Moon.

The creation of "For You" came at a significant cost, exceeding Prince's initial advance. To manage his growing musical empire, he established the Prince's Music Co. to publish his songs. The album's single "Soft and Wet" found its place on the music charts, reaching No. 12 on the Hot Soul Singles chart and No. 92 on the Billboard Hot 100. Additionally, the track "Just as Long as We're Together" achieved No. 91 on the Hot Soul Singles chart, signifying the emergence of a musical force that was destined for greatness.

The year 1979 marked a pivotal moment in Prince's career, as he assembled a band that would soon become an essential part of his musical journey. André Cymone held down the bass, Dez Dickerson wielded the guitar, and the ensemble was further enriched by Gayle Chapman and Doctor Fink on keyboards, with Bobby Z. providing the driving beat on drums. Their debut performance unfolded on January 5, 1979, at the Capri Theater, a momentous occasion attended by Warner Bros. executives who keenly observed their burgeoning talent.

Despite their undeniable potential, the label felt that Prince and his band needed more time to evolve their distinctive sound. Yet, Prince was not deterred. In October 1979, he unleashed the eponymous album "Prince." This release made a resounding impact, reaching No. 4 on the Billboard Top R&B/Black Albums chart and No. 22 on the Billboard 200. "Prince" swiftly achieved platinum status, a testament to the artist's burgeoning popularity.

The album was graced by two R&B hits, "Why You Wanna Treat Me So Bad?" and "I Wanna Be Your Lover." The latter track, in particular, resonated with audiences, selling over a million copies and ascending to No. 11 on the Billboard Hot 100. On the Hot Soul Singles chart, it achieved the pinnacle position, staying at No. 1 for two weeks. These hits took center stage on the iconic American Bandstand stage on January 26, 1980, as Prince mesmerized the audience with his electric performance.

Throughout this period, Prince utilized Ecnirp Music – BMI, solidifying his place as a prolific composer and performer.

In 1980, Prince continued his musical odyssey with the release of the album "Dirty Mind." This album was a striking departure from convention, brimming with sexually explicit material. Songs like the title track "Dirty Mind," "Head," and

"Sister" were audacious blends of funk, new wave, R&B, and pop, characterized by their unabashedly salacious themes and a penchant for shock value. Recorded within the confines of Prince's personal studio, the album was met with widespread acclaim, achieving gold certification.

One of the album's standout tracks, "Uptown," captured the essence of the era, reaching No. 5 on the Billboard Dance chart and also climbing to No. 5 on the Hot Soul Singles chart. Beyond his studio work, Prince took to the stage as the opening act for Rick James' 1980 "Fire It Up" tour, solidifying his reputation as a dynamic live performer and an artist unafraid to push the boundaries of artistic expression.

February of 1981 marked a significant milestone in Prince's career as he made his inaugural appearance on the iconic television show "Saturday Night Live." The electrifying performance featured "Partyup," setting the stage for his meteoric rise.

In October 1981, Prince once again enthralled his fans with the release of the album "Controversy." As an artist unafraid to explore the boundaries of expression, he embarked on a journey to support this album. A noteworthy chapter unfolded when he joined the legendary Rolling Stones as the first of three opening acts on their U.S. tour. This particular episode in Los Angeles took an unexpected turn as Prince, clad in a trench coat and black bikini briefs, faced a barrage of audience members throwing trash at him, resulting in his early exit from the stage.

The dawn of 1982 witnessed Prince headlining a small tour of college towns, reaffirming his prowess as a live performer.

"Controversy" was notable not only for its musical content but also for the introduction of Prince's unique abbreviated spelling. He gave birth to his own lexicon, using "U" instead of "you," "2" instead of "to," and "4" instead of "for." This distinct style of expression would continue to evolve and become a hallmark of his artistic identity, extending into his album titles, liner notes, and online presence.

In 1981, Prince was a man of many talents and initiated a side project band known as "The Time." This band, a creative laboratory for his musical genius, released four albums between 1981 and 1990. Prince played a central role in writing and performing most of the instrumentation and backing vocals for the group, occasionally credited under the pseudonyms "Jamie Starr" or "The Starr Company." The lead vocals were masterfully handled by Morris Day, further illustrating the breadth of Prince's musical dexterity.

In late 1982, Prince unveiled a double album that would become a monumental success - "1999." This opus resonated with audiences, selling over four million copies. The album's title track, "1999," was not merely a musical sensation; it was also a protest against nuclear proliferation, galvanizing Prince's stance on social and political issues. This anthem became his first top 10 hit outside the United States.

"Little Red Corvette," another jewel from the album, achieved a remarkable feat by becoming one of the first two videos by black artists to receive extensive airplay on MTV, alongside Michael Jackson's "Billie Jean." This achievement was particularly noteworthy as MTV had been previously criticized for not adequately representing "black music" in its programming. In response to this oversight, CBS President Walter Yetnikoff threatened to withdraw all CBS videos, leading to a pivotal shift in the network's approach.

The musical landscape of the early 1980s witnessed a competitive rivalry between Prince and Michael Jackson. This rivalry, fueled by their musical prowess and star power, would persist for many years, creating an electrifying dynamic in the world of music.

The song "Delirious" from the "1999" album also made its mark, climbing to the top ten on the Billboard Hot 100 chart. Additionally, "International Lover" garnered Prince his first Grammy Award nomination at the 26th Annual Grammy Awards, a testament to the depth and diversity of his musical talents.

1984–1987: PURPLE REIGN AND GLOBAL DOMINANCE

The period from 1984 to 1987 was a transformative chapter in Prince's career, marked by his association with a band he referred to as "the Revolution." Their name was creatively printed, in reverse, on the cover of the "1999" album, ingeniously nestled inside the letter "I" of the word "Prince." The ensemble consisted of Lisa Coleman and Doctor Fink on keyboards, Bobby Z. on drums, Brown Mark on bass, and Dez Dickerson on guitar. Jill Jones, a gifted backing singer, was also part of the lineup for the "1999" album and subsequent tour.

However, following the "1999 Tour," Dez Dickerson made the decision to depart from the group, citing religious reasons and a desire to explore other musical avenues. In his place, Wendy Melvoin, a close friend of Lisa Coleman, joined the Revolution, and her addition would become a pivotal moment in the band's history.

At the time, Prince's ambitions extended far beyond the boundaries of the music world. In the early 1980s, he set his sights on the silver screen, insisting that his management secure a deal for him to star in a major motion picture. This vision would culminate in the release of the hit film "Purple Rain" in 1984. The film, loosely autobiographical and starring Prince himself, would not only become a cultural phenomenon but also have a profound impact on his career.

The eponymous studio album "Purple Rain," serving as the film's soundtrack, achieved remarkable success. It sold over 13 million copies in the United States and dominated the Billboard 200 chart for an astonishing 24 consecutive weeks. The film, in a triumphant moment, earned Prince an Academy Award for Best Original Song Score and grossed over $68 million in the US.

Songs from the film, such as "When Doves Cry" and "Let's Go Crazy," soared to the top of pop charts worldwide, reaching No. 1. The title track, "Purple Rain," held the No. 2 position on the Billboard Hot 100. In a remarkable display of his influence, Prince achieved the extraordinary feat of simultaneously holding the No. 1 album, single, and film in the United States in 1984, a historic milestone for a musician.

The "Purple Rain" album's impact extended beyond its time, with Rolling Stone ranking it as the 8th of the "500 Greatest Albums of All Time." Time magazine also recognized its significance, including it in the list of the "All-Time 100 Albums." Additionally, the album secured two of Prince's first three Grammy Awards, earned at the 27th Annual Grammy Awards, in the categories of

Best Rock Performance by a Duo or Group with Vocal and Best Score Soundtrack for Visual Media. This period solidified Prince's status as a global icon and a musical force to be reckoned with.

In 1984, the world of art and music intersected as pop art luminary Andy Warhol turned his gaze toward Prince. The result of this fascination was the creation of a remarkable painting titled "Orange Prince" in 1984. Warhol's captivation with Prince extended beyond a single canvas, and he ultimately produced a total of twelve unique paintings of the iconic musician, each adorned with different color schemes. These extraordinary works of art found a home in Warhol's personal collection.

The enduring legacy of this artistic collaboration is underscored by the fact that four of these unique paintings are now housed in The Andy Warhol Museum in Pittsburgh. In November 1984, the world was treated to a visual representation of Prince's unparalleled influence as Warhol's portrait of the artist graced the pages of Vanity Fair. This iconic image accompanied an article entitled "Purple Fame" by Tristan Fox. The article, accompanied by Warhol's silkscreen image, aptly captured Prince "at the height of his powers." It was a critical appreciation that marked a significant moment in Prince's career, coinciding with the commencement of the 98-date "Purple Rain Tour."

In the same year, Prince found himself at the center of a cultural and political storm when Tipper Gore, mother of an 11-year-old named Karenna, heard her daughter listening to Prince's controversial song "Darling Nikki." The song had garnered widespread notoriety for its explicit and sexually suggestive lyrics, including a reference to masturbation. In response to this, Tipper Gore founded the Parents Music Resource Center, a group that advocated for the mandatory use of warning labels on record covers, specifically the "Parental Advisory: Explicit Lyrics" label, on albums containing content deemed unsuitable for minors. The music industry eventually heeded this call and voluntarily implemented the labeling system.

In 1985, Prince made a surprising announcement that sent shockwaves through the music world. He declared his intention to discontinue live performances and music videos following the release of his next album. The album in question, "Around the World in a Day," was released that same year and promptly climbed to the No. 1 spot on the Billboard 200, maintaining its position for three consecutive weeks. The album produced the hit single "Raspberry Beret," which reached No. 2 on the Billboard Hot 100, and "Pop Life," which secured the No. 7 spot on the charts. This period marked a turning point in Prince's career as he continued to evolve as a musician and cultural icon.

The year 1986 brought more musical triumphs and cinematic adventures into Prince's life. His album "Parade" soared to No. 3 on the Billboard 200 chart and claimed the No. 2 spot on the R&B charts. The album boasted a stellar track, "Kiss," for which the video was masterfully choreographed by Louis Falco. "Kiss" soon became a chart-topping sensation, securing the No. 1 position on the Billboard Hot 100. Remarkably, this catchy hit was originally penned for a side project called Mazarati, underscoring Prince's prolific songwriting talent.

During the same year, another one of Prince's compositions made waves when the song "Manic Monday," written by him and performed by the Bangles, reached the No. 2 position on the Hot 100 chart. This string of musical successes was a testament to Prince's remarkable ability to craft songs that resonated with audiences across genres.

The album "Parade" not only graced the airwaves but also served as the soundtrack for Prince's second foray into filmmaking, "Under the Cherry Moon," released in 1986. In this film, Prince took on the roles of both director and lead actor, a project that also featured Kristin Scott Thomas. While the "Parade" album achieved platinum status and sold an impressive two million copies, the film "Under the Cherry Moon" had a different fate. It was honored with a Golden Raspberry Award for Worst Picture, tied with "Howard the Duck." Prince himself was the recipient of multiple Golden Raspberry Awards, earning distinctions for Worst Director, Worst Actor, and Worst Original Song (for the track "Love or Money").

In 1986, Prince embarked on a remarkable series of live performances known as the "Hit n Run - Parade Tour." This tour was a testament to his dynamic stage presence and drew audiences into his musical world. Following the tour, Prince made significant changes to his band. He disbanded the Revolution and parted ways with Wendy & Lisa. Brown Mark also left the band, but keyboardist Doctor Fink remained. To fill the void, Prince recruited new and talented band members, including Miko Weaver on guitar, Atlanta Bliss on trumpet, and Eric Leeds on saxophone. This transformative period marked a chapter of reinvention and evolution in Prince's career.

1987–1991: MUSICAL EXPLORATIONS AND CINEMATIC VENTURES

The period spanning from 1987 to 1991 was marked by significant changes and musical experimentation in Prince's career. Prior to the disbanding of the Revolution, Prince had been concurrently working on two distinct projects: the Revolution album "Dream Factory" and a solo effort under the moniker "Camille." Unlike their previous collaborative albums, "Dream Factory" saw greater input from the band members, even featuring songs with lead vocals by Wendy & Lisa. Meanwhile, the "Camille" project introduced a new androgynous persona for Prince, who primarily sang in a sped-up, female-sounding voice.

With the departure of the Revolution, Prince was left with an abundance of unreleased material from both "Dream Factory" and "Camille," alongside some fresh compositions. These resources coalesced into a grand vision for a three-LP album, initially titled "Crystal Ball." However, Warner Bros. Records insisted on reducing the ambitious triple album to a double album, ultimately resulting in the release of "Sign o' the Times" on March 31, 1987.

"Sign o' the Times" swiftly made its mark, ascending to No. 6 on the Billboard 200 albums chart. The album's title track, "Sign o' the Times," charted at No. 3 on the Hot 100, earning critical acclaim and capturing the essence of its era. The follow-up single, "If I Was Your Girlfriend," charted at No. 67 on the Hot 100 but surged to No. 12 on the R&B chart. Another hit came in the form of a duet with Sheena Easton, "U Got the Look," which achieved a remarkable No. 2 ranking on the Hot 100 and No. 11 on the R&B chart. The album's final single, "I Could Never Take the Place of Your Man," concluded its chart journey at No. 10 on the

Hot 100 and No. 14 on the R&B chart. These singles showcased the diversity of Prince's musical style and his unique ability to connect with audiences across various genres.

"Sign o' the Times" was not only a commercial success but also earned critical acclaim, becoming the top album of the year according to the Pazz & Jop critics' poll. The album achieved sales of 3.2 million copies. In Europe, it enjoyed considerable popularity, leading Prince to promote the album overseas with an extensive tour.

As he embarked on this new chapter, Prince assembled a fresh backing band, recruiting members from the remnants of the Revolution. The new lineup included bassist Levi Seacer Jr., keyboardist Boni Boyer, and dancer/choreographer Cat Glover. They joined forces with new drummer Sheila E and the existing musicians from the Revolution era, including Miko Weaver, Doctor

Fink, Eric Leeds, Atlanta Bliss, and the Bodyguards (Jerome, Wally Safford, and Greg Brooks). Together, this dynamic ensemble embarked on the "Sign o' the Times Tour," marking another captivating phase in Prince's live performances.

The "Sign o' the Times" tour was a resounding success overseas, and both Warner Bros. and Prince's management were eager to bring it to the United States to further boost album sales. However, Prince had a different vision. He was eager to dive into the creative process of producing a new album, which led to a reluctance to embark on a full-fledged US tour. To strike a compromise, it was decided that the last two nights of the tour would be filmed for eventual release in movie theaters. Yet, the initial quality of the film was deemed subpar, prompting reshoots at Prince's own Paisley Park studios. The revamped film, titled "Sign o' the Times," was released on November 20, 1987. This cinematic production garnered better reviews than "Under the Cherry Moon," Prince's previous film, but it faced limited success at the box office and had a brief run in theaters.

Prince's next planned album was "The Black Album," which marked a departure from recent releases. It delved into instrumental compositions and embraced a funk and R&B theme, with Prince even experimenting with hip hop on tracks like "Bob George" and "Dead on It." The album was initially intended to have a monochromatic black cover with only the catalog number printed. Approximately 500,000 copies had been pressed when Prince had a spiritual awakening and decided that the album was tainted with negative energy. He subsequently ordered its recall. "The Black Album" did eventually see the light of day, but it was released by Warner Bros. as a limited edition album in 1994.

In response to this creative shift, Prince returned to the studio for eight weeks and crafted "Lovesexy," which was released on May 10, 1988. This album served as a spiritual counterpoint to the dark and enigmatic "The Black Album." Every track on "Lovesexy" was a solo effort by Prince, except for "Eye No," which he recorded with his backing band at the time. The album reached No. 11 on the Billboard 200 and No. 5 on the R&B albums chart. The lead single, "Alphabet St.," reached No. 8 on the Hot 100 and No. 3 on the R&B chart, with sales of 750,000 copies.

Prince once again took his post-Revolution backing band, minus the Bodyguards, on an extensive "Lovesexy World Tour." This tour, comprising 84 shows across three legs, was met with immense enthusiasm from large audiences. However, the elaborate sets and props used in the shows made it challenging to turn a net profit, despite the positive reception from fans.

In 1989, Prince made a notable appearance on Madonna's studio album "Like a Prayer." He co-wrote and sang the duet "Love Song" with Madonna and played electric guitar (though uncredited) on several other tracks, including "Like a Prayer," "Keep It Together," and "Act of Contrition." During this time, he also commenced work on several musical projects, such as "Rave Unto the Joy Fantastic" and early drafts of his film "Graffiti Bridge." However, both of these projects were put on hold when he received a request from Tim Burton, the director of the 1989 film "Batman," to record several songs for the upcoming live-action adaptation.

Prince wholeheartedly embraced the opportunity and went into the studio, resulting in the creation of an entire nine-track album. Warner Bros. released this album, titled "Batman," on June 20, 1989. The album reached the No. 1 spot on the

Billboard 200 chart and sold 4.3 million copies. The single "Batdance" from the album claimed the top positions on the Billboard Hot 100 and R&B charts.

Additionally, the single "The Arms of Orion," a duet with Sheena Easton, reached No. 36 on the charts, while "Partyman," which also featured the vocals of Prince's then-girlfriend (nicknamed Anna Fantastic), secured the No. 18 position on the Hot 100 and the No. 5 spot on the R&B chart. The love ballad "Scandalous!" peaked at No. 5 on the R&B chart. As part of the deal to create the "Batman" soundtrack, Prince had to relinquish all publishing rights to the songs on the album to Warner Bros.

In 1990, Prince embarked on his Nude Tour, featuring a revamped band lineup. This tour showcased a back-to-basics approach, with the departures of several previous band members like Boni Boyer, Sheila E., the horn section, and Cat.

New additions included keyboardist Rosie Gaines, drummer Michael Bland, and the dancing trio known as the Game Boyz (Tony M., Kirky J., and Damon Dickson). The tour was a financial success during its European and Japanese legs, offering a concise greatest hits setlist.

As the year unfolded, Prince also completed production on his fourth film, "Graffiti Bridge" (1990), and released an album with the same title. Initially, Warner Bros. had reservations about funding the film, but they gave it the green light after Prince assured them it would serve as a sequel to "Purple Rain" and with the involvement of the original members of the Time. The "Graffiti Bridge" album, released on August 20, 1990, reached No. 6 on the Billboard 200 and the R&B albums chart. The single "Thieves in the Temple" reached No. 6 on the Hot 100 and claimed the No. 1 position on the R&B chart, while "Round and Round" secured the No. 12 spot on the US charts and No. 2 on the R&B charts. Notably, "Round and Round" featured the teenage Tevin Campbell on lead vocals.

However, the "Graffiti Bridge" film, released on November 20, 1990, did not perform as well, earning only $4.2 million at the box office. After the release of both the film and the album, the remaining members of the Revolution, Miko Weaver and Doctor Fink, departed from Prince's band.

1991–1996: A TIME OF TRANSFORMATION AND INNOVATION

In the early '90s, Prince was on a new musical journey with his band, the New Power Generation. This lineup brought together both fresh faces and familiar ones from his previous bands. Among the new additions were guitarist Levi Seacer, bassist Sonny T., keyboardist Tommy Barbarella, and a talented brass section known as the Hornheads. They joined forces with existing members like Rosie Gaines, Michael Bland, and the Game Boyz.

It was during this period that Prince crafted his album "Diamonds and Pearls," and it was clear that his band members played a crucial role in shaping the music. Released on October 1, 1991, this album achieved significant success, reaching No. 3 on the prestigious Billboard 200 chart. The tracks from this record became memorable hits, painting a vivid musical landscape.

The sultry "Gett Off" oozed with energy, climbing to No. 21 on the Hot 100 and No. 6 on the R&B charts. "Cream" was an absolute triumph, marking Prince's fifth US No. 1 single. The title track, "Diamonds and Pearls," was a sensual masterpiece that reached No. 3 on the Hot 100 and dominated the R&B charts. "Money Don't Matter 2 Night" captured hearts, attaining No. 23 on the Hot 100 and No. 14 on the R&B charts.

As the calendar flipped to 1992, Prince was poised to release his 14th studio album. This record, featuring the New Power Generation, bore a cryptic, unpronounceable symbol on the cover, later recognized as "Love Symbol #2." This symbol was a fusion of the male ($\male$) and female ($\female$) icons, signifying his unique artistic identity. The album's title became something of a puzzle, and it alluded to a captivating story of self-expression.

Prince had a vision for his first single, "My Name Is Prince," which he believed would resonate with the audience he had cultivated through his previous work. This track resonated with its 'hip-hoppery,' but it reached only No. 36 on the Billboard Hot 100 and No. 23 on the R&B chart. The follow-up single, "Sexy MF," added a spicy touch to the mix, charting at No. 66 on the Hot 100 and No. 76 on the R&B chart. However, the track "7" resonated deeply with fans, reaching an impressive No. 7 on the charts.

The album, often affectionately referred to as "Love Symbol," ascended to No. 5 on the Billboard 200 chart and showcased Prince's unparalleled ability to fuse various musical elements. With 2.8 million copies sold worldwide, it was a testament to his musical evolution.

In 1993, Prince faced some obstacles with his record label, Warner Bros., as they had been reluctant to release his vast backlog of music at the pace he desired. Frustrated by this, Prince took a bold step and officially adopted the "Love Symbol" as his stage name, a move that would come to symbolize his struggle for artistic control and independence. To incorporate this unique symbol in print media, Warner Bros. organized a mass distribution of floppy disks containing a custom font for this symbol.

During this period, he became widely known as "the Artist Formerly Known as Prince" or simply "the Artist." This symbolically and literally separated him from the confines of a traditional name, reflecting his determination to break free from industry constraints.

Prince, determined to assert more control over his musical career and escape the limitations imposed by Warner Bros., began releasing albums in quick succession. He used this strategy as a means to fulfill his contractual obligations and regain creative autonomy. He even took the bold step of appearing with the word "slave" written on his face as a protest against what he saw as the label's oppressive influence.

He was convinced that Warner Bros. had hindered the commercial success of his album "Love Symbol" by not promoting it adequately. It was during this time that the once-abandoned "The Black Album" was officially released, seven years after its initial recording. Interestingly, the "new" release had already been widely distributed as a bootleg. Eventually, Warner Bros. yielded to Prince's demands and released an album of his new material titled "Come." This marked a turning point in his career as he continued to fight for his artistic freedom and control over his work.

Prince's determination to maintain control over his music production and release strategy persisted. He pushed for the simultaneous release of his next album, "The Gold Experience," alongside the Love Symbol-era material. Warner Bros., however, was cautious and allowed only the single "The Most Beautiful Girl in the World" to be released through a small, independent distributor called Bellmark Records in February 1994.

"The Most Beautiful Girl in the World" quickly gained popularity, reaching No. 3 on the US Billboard Hot 100 and claiming the No. 1 spot in many other countries. Despite its success, this approach didn't set a precedent for future releases. Warner Bros. continued to resist releasing "The Gold Experience," citing concerns over potential poor sales and arguing that the market was already saturated.

Finally, in September 1995, "The Gold Experience" was made available to the public, initially reaching the top 10 of the Billboard 200. However, the album is no longer in print due to an ongoing legal case related to "The Most Beautiful Girl in the World." Digital distributors have excluded this disputed song from the album.

In a significant development, an Italian court ruled in 2003 that "The Most Beautiful Girl in the World" had plagiarized the song "Takin' Me to Paradise" by Bruno Bergonzi and Michele Vicino. Bergonzi and Vicino won their case on appeal in 2007. The final verdict came from the Court of Cassation of Rome in May 2015, but the international legal battle continues. The Italian collecting society SIAE officially recognizes Bergonzi and Vicino as the authors of the music for "The Most Beautiful Girl in the World."

Prince's relationship with Warner Bros. was strained, and in 1996, he released "Chaos and Disorder," which marked his final album of new material under his contract with Warner Bros. Unfortunately, this release proved to be one of his least commercially successful albums.

1996–2000: EXPLORING NEW HORIZONS AND COLLABORATIONS

In 1996, after Prince had fulfilled his contractual obligations with Warner Bros., he embarked on a major comeback. He unleashed his creative energy with the release of "Emancipation," a groundbreaking 3-CD set featuring a total of 36 songs, with each disc clocking in at precisely 60 minutes. This ambitious project was released under his independent label, NPG Records, with distribution through EMI. Notably, for publishing his songs on "Emancipation," Prince opted to use "Emancipated Music Inc. - ASCAP," breaking from his long-standing use of "Controversy Music - ASCAP" dating back to 1981.

"Emancipation" achieved Platinum certification from the RIAA and marked the first time Prince included covers of other artists' songs on his record. These tracks included Joan Osborne's hit "One of Us," "Betcha by Golly Wow!" by Thom Bell and Linda Creed, "I Can't Make You Love Me" by James Allen Shamblin II and Michael Barry Reid, and "La-La (Means I Love You)" by Thom Bell and William Hart.

Prince followed "Emancipation" with the release of "Crystal Ball" in 1998, a five-CD compilation featuring previously unreleased material.

However, the distribution of this album was somewhat chaotic, with fans pre-ordering the album on his website up to a year before receiving it. "Crystal Ball" was eventually available in retail stores, with a retail edition containing only four of the five discs, omitting the Kamasutra disc. There were two different packaging editions, one with a white cover and the Love Symbol in a colored circle on a four-disc sized jewel case and the other featuring a round translucent snap jewel case that held all four discs. The music content was the same in both versions.

Within three months, Prince released the album "Newpower Soul." During the same period, he collaborated on Chaka Khan's "Come 2 My House" and Larry Graham's "GCS2000," both of which were released on the NPG label. These projects received promotion through live appearances, including spots on "Vibe with Sinbad" and the NBC Today show's Summer Concert Series.

In 1999, Prince signed with another major label, Arista Records, for the release of a new album, "Rave Un2 the Joy Fantastic." Prior to this, Warner Bros. had also released "The Vault: Old Friends 4 Sale," a collection of unreleased material spanning Prince's career.

The year 1999 concluded with a spectacular pay-per-view concert event, "Rave Un2 the Year 2000," which was broadcast on December 31, 1999. It featured footage from Prince's December 17 and 18 concerts during his 1999 tour. The concert included guest appearances by musicians such as Lenny Kravitz, George Clinton, Jimmy Russell, and The Time. Following the broadcast, it was released on home video in the subsequent year.

2000–2007: RETURN TO CHART-TOPPING SUCCESS

The year 2000 marked a pivotal moment in Prince's career. Fueled by his desire for artistic freedom and contractual obligations that had finally concluded, he made a significant announcement. On May 16, 2000, he officially retired the Love Symbol as his name, a symbol that had become synonymous with him. He expressed that his decision was rooted in the need to break free from the negative associations tied to the name "Prince."

However, it's worth noting that the Love Symbol continued to feature prominently in his work. Although his name had changed, he still utilized the iconic symbol as a logo, embellishing album artwork and even playing a guitar in the shape of the Love Symbol. Despite the change in his official name, he retained a strong connection to this beloved emblem.

During the years following his transformation, Prince opted to release much of his new music through his Internet subscription service. This service initially went by the name NPGOnlineLtd.com but later rebranded as NPGMusicClub.com. This approach offered fans a unique way to access his music. Some of the notable albums that emerged during this period included "Rave In2 the Joy Fantastic" (2001), "The Rainbow Children" (2001), "One Nite Alone..." (2002), "Xpectation" (2003), "C-Note" (2004), "The Chocolate Invasion" (2004), and "The Slaughterhouse" (2004).

In 2001, Warner Bros. released a compilation album called "The Very Best of Prince." This collection encompassed many of his commercially successful singles from the 1980s, allowing fans to relive his classic hits. A year later, Prince delivered his first live album, "One Nite Alone... Live!" The album featured performances from the One Nite Alone... Tour, granting his fans the opportunity to experience his live shows from the comfort of their homes. The 3-CD box set also included a unique twist—a disc of "aftershow" music entitled "It Ain't Over!" This captured the essence of his live performances, where the music and energy extended beyond the main show.

During this time, Prince was determined to establish deeper connections with his fan base. He achieved this through the NPG Music Club, which facilitated closer interactions. Fans were invited to tour his iconic studio, engage in interviews, participate in discussions, and enjoy listening sessions with his music. It was a unique opportunity for fans to get closer to the artist behind the music, offering a level of engagement that was truly special.

In 2004, Prince was not only a presence at the 46th Annual Grammy Awards but also shared the stage with the incomparable Beyoncé. Their opening performance was nothing short of spectacular, a medley featuring "Purple Rain," "Let's Go Crazy," "Baby I'm a Star," and Beyoncé's "Crazy in Love." The electrifying performance set the stage for the evening.

The Grammy Awards also marked a momentous occasion as Prince was inducted into the Rock and Roll Hall of Fame, a testament to his unparalleled impact on music. During the ceremony, he received this honor from Alicia Keys, as well as Big Boi and André 3000 of OutKast. But Prince wasn't just there to accept an award; he was there to perform. He graced the audience with a thrilling trio of his hits, delivering an unforgettable performance.

However, what stole the show was his contribution to a tribute to the legendary George Harrison, a fellow inductee. During their rendition of "While My Guitar Gently Weeps," Prince's guitar solo was nothing short of awe-inspiring, a mesmerizing two-minute display of his unparalleled talent. It was a moment that left a lasting impression on those in attendance, cementing his status as a musical legend.

Even as he continued to evolve and experiment with his music, Prince remained deeply connected to his musical influences. He paid tribute to the legendary Jimi Hendrix by performing "Red House," putting his own unique spin on it and aptly naming it "Purple House."

In April 2004, Prince unveiled "Musicology" under a one-album agreement with Columbia, marking a significant moment in his illustrious career. The album rapidly climbed the charts, reaching the top five in numerous countries, including the United States, the United Kingdom, Germany, and Australia. One notable factor that contributed to its chart success in the US was a clever move: every CD was bundled with concert tickets. This innovative strategy, in accordance with chart rules at the time, allowed each CD sold in this manner to count towards its US chart ranking.

Just three months later, Prince received an extraordinary accolade when Spin magazine declared him the greatest frontman of all time. His magnetic stage presence and electrifying performances had solidified his status as an unparalleled live performer.

During the same year, Rolling Stone magazine crowned Prince as the highest-earning musician globally, with an annual income of a staggering $56.5 million. This financial triumph was primarily attributed to his successful "Musicology Tour," recognized by Pollstar as the leading concert attraction in the United States. This tour saw Prince taking the stage for a total of 96 concerts, with an average ticket price of $61 (equivalent to approximately $95 in 2022).

Prince's "Musicology" album earned critical acclaim and secured two Grammy awards, one for Best Male R&B Vocal Performance for "Call My Name" and another for Best Traditional R&B Vocal Performance for the album's title track. Furthermore, "Musicology" received nominations for Best R&B Song and Best R&B Album, while the track "Cinnamon Girl" earned a nomination for Best Male Pop Vocal Performance. Rolling Stone magazine acknowledged his enduring influence by ranking Prince at No. 27 on their list of the 100 Greatest Artists of All Time.

In April 2005, Prince graced Stevie Wonder's single "So What the Fuss" with his exceptional guitar skills, collaborating with En Vogue who provided the backing vocals. This single marked Wonder's first release since 1999, and Prince's contribution added a distinctive touch to this long-awaited return.

Later in 2005, Prince inked a deal with Universal Music for the release of his album "3121," which hit the shelves on March 21, 2006. "Te Amo Corazón" was the first single, and its music video was directed by the talented actress Salma Hayek. Filmed in the enchanting backdrop of Marrakech, Morocco, the video featured Argentine actress and singer Mía Maestro. The second single, "Black Sweat," made waves at the MTV VMAs and was nominated for Best Cinematography.

The immediate success of "3121" was a career milestone for Prince, marking his first No. 1 debut on the Billboard 200. This achievement underlined his enduring musical prowess and his continued relevance in the music industry.

To promote the release of "3121," Prince made a memorable appearance on Saturday Night Live on February 4, 2006, after 17 years since his last SNL performance at the 15th-anniversary special and almost 25 years since his initial appearance on a regular episode in 1981.

Prince's innovative use of the Internet to connect with his audience and distribute his music didn't go unnoticed. In June 2006, at the Webby Awards, he received a prestigious Webby Lifetime Achievement Award. This award celebrated his visionary approach to using the Internet to reach his fans and deliver his music, a prime example being his exclusive online release of the album "Crystal Ball" in 1998. His pioneering efforts paved the way for many artists to engage with their audiences in new and groundbreaking ways.

In July 2006, Prince made a surprising move by shutting down his NPG Music Club website, which had been in operation for more than five years. This decision came just weeks after he had won a Webby Award, celebrating his innovative use of the internet to distribute music and connect with his fans. On the very day of the music club's closure, an unexpected twist occurred. Prince found himself facing a lawsuit from the British company HM Publishing, owners of the Nature Publishing Group, also known as NPG. While these events coincided on the same day, Prince's attorney clarified that the site's closure was unrelated to the trademark dispute with the company.

Throughout 2006, Prince remained a prominent figure in the music scene, making notable appearances at various award ceremonies. On February 15, he graced the stage at the 2006 Brit

Awards, performing alongside Wendy & Lisa and Sheila E. Later, on June 27, Prince was a key figure at the 2006 BET Awards, where he received the prestigious award for Best Male R&B Artist. He also delivered a mesmerizing medley of Chaka Khan's songs to celebrate Khan's BET Lifetime Achievement Award.

In the same year, Prince was approached to voice the character of the Prince XII cat in the film "Garfield: A Tail of Two Kitties." However, for reasons unknown, he stepped down from the role, and actor Tim Curry took over the part.

November 2006 was a momentous month for Prince. He was honored with an induction into the UK Music Hall of Fame, a significant recognition of his lasting impact on the world of music. Although he accepted the award, he did not perform at the ceremony. Around the same time, in November 2006, Prince ventured into the nightlife scene by opening a nightclub called "3121" in Las Vegas, located at the Rio All Suite Hotel and Casino. He delighted fans with performances every Friday and Saturday night, keeping the party going until April 2007 when his contract with the Rio came to a close.

As his career continued to thrive, Prince released "Ultimate Prince" on August 22, 2006. This double-disc collection included a CD featuring his previous hits and another showcasing extended versions and mixes of tracks that had predominantly been available only as vinyl record B-sides.

In the realm of film, Prince made his mark in the animated hit "Happy Feet" in 2006. He wrote and performed the song "The Song of the Heart," which was featured on the film's soundtrack. Notably, the soundtrack also included a cover of Prince's earlier hit "Kiss," sung by Nicole Kidman and Hugh

Jackman. This stellar contribution earned "The Song of the Heart" a Golden Globe Award for Best Original Song in January 2007.

2007–2010: UNFORGETTABLE PERFORMANCES AND MUSICAL VENTURES

The year 2007 brought one of Prince's most iconic and memorable performances as he took center stage at Super Bowl XLI's halftime show in Miami, Florida. Performing on a grand stage cleverly shaped like his iconic symbol, he wowed the audience of a staggering 140 million television viewers, marking one of the largest audiences he had ever played for. Despite the rain, Prince delivered a sensational 12-minute performance that began with a captivating intro featuring the Queen song "We Will Rock You" and concluded with his iconic "Purple Rain" rendition. In the annals of

Super Bowl history, this performance secured a special place. In 2015, Billboard even ranked it as the greatest Super Bowl performance ever.

During his Earth Tour in mid-2007, Prince showcased his incredible talent in London, playing an astounding 21 concerts at the O2 Arena. What set this tour apart was Prince's gesture of capping ticket prices at just £31.21 ($48.66), making his music accessible to a wide range of fans. With legendary saxophonist Maceo Parker joining his band, the demand for his performances was staggering. After all 140,000 tickets for the original seven concerts sold out within 20 minutes, Prince extended his residency at the O2 Arena to a total of 21 nights.

In the same year, Prince teamed up with Sheila E. to deliver a mesmerizing performance at the 2007 ALMA Awards. Additionally, on June 28, 2007, a surprising move was made by the Mail on Sunday when they announced a groundbreaking deal. They declared that Prince's new album, "Planet Earth," would be given away for free with their newspaper, making it the first place in the world to access the album. This bold decision stirred controversy among music distributors and led Sony BMG, Prince's distributor, to withdraw the album from UK stores. Despite this, the UK's largest high street music retailer, HMV, decided to stock the paper on release day to meet the demand from fans.

On July 7, 2007, Prince returned to his hometown, Minneapolis, for a series of spectacular performances. He graced the stage at various venues, including the Macy's Auditorium to promote his new perfume "3121" on Nicollet Mall, the Target Center arena, and First Avenue. The First Avenue performance was especially significant as it marked his first appearance at the venue since 1987. This historic club was famously featured in the film "Purple Rain," further adding to the significance of the event.

In 2008, Prince welcomed a new chapter in his career with Kiran Sharma, a UK-based manager who took on the role of managing his affairs. The artist continued to captivate audiences with his music, showcasing his ever-evolving talents. On April 25, 2008, Prince graced "The Tonight Show with Jay Leno," where he unveiled a brand new track, "Turn Me Loose," thrilling fans with his innovative sound.

Notably, Prince headlined the 2008 Coachella Festival, leaving an indelible mark on the event. His performance came at a considerable cost, with Reuters reporting that he received more than $5 million for his appearance. In an unexpected turn of events, Prince canceled a concert scheduled at Dublin's Croke Park with just 10 days' notice. This abrupt cancellation led to a legal battle, as in

October 2009, the concert promoters, MCD Productions, filed a lawsuit against Prince, seeking €1.6 million as a refund for 55,126 tickets. Eventually, the case was settled out of court in February 2010, with Prince agreeing to pay $2.95 million.

During the legal proceedings, it came to light that Prince had been offered a staggering $22 million for seven concerts as part of a proposed 2008 European tour. This revelation highlighted his immense drawing power and the demand for his electrifying performances.

In October 2008, Prince gifted his fans with a live album titled "Indigo Nights." This collection featured songs performed live at aftershows in the IndigO2, showcasing his incredible stage presence.

In December 2008, Prince took a new musical direction, premiering four songs from his upcoming album on LA's Indie rock radio station, Indie 103.1. The radio station's programmers were invited to Prince's residence, where he personally handed them a CD with the four songs to be premiered on their show "Jonesy's Jukebox," hosted by former Sex Pistol Steve Jones.

On January 3, 2009, Prince launched a new website, LotusFlow3r.com. This platform offered fans the opportunity to stream and purchase recently aired material and concert tickets. Prince's commitment to innovative digital distribution was evident when he released two more songs, "Disco Jellyfish" and "Another Boy," on the website just a few weeks later. More tracks, including "Chocolate Box," "Colonized Mind," and "All This Love," were subsequently released.

The prolific artist didn't stop there. On March 24, 2009, Prince gifted his fans a remarkable triple album set comprising "Lotusflower," "MPLSoUND," and an album credited to Bria Valente titled "Elixer." This triple album release was followed by a physical release on March 29, ensuring that his music was accessible in various formats.

Further cementing his status as a legendary performer, Prince graced the Montreux Jazz Festival on July 18, 2009, delivering two extraordinary shows. Backed by the New Power Generation, which included talented musicians like Rhonda Smith, Renato Neto, and John Blackwell, Prince left an indelible mark on the renowned festival. Later in the year, he continued to surprise audiences with impromptu performances at venues like the Grand Palais on October 11 and La Cigale on October 12. On October 24, 2009, Prince held a memorable concert at his own Paisley Park, where fans were once again treated to his unparalleled musical prowess.

2010–2016: FINAL ALBUMS

As the calendar turned to 2010, Prince continued to weave his musical magic. In January of that year, he composed a fresh tune titled "Purple and Gold," inspired by his visit to a Minnesota Vikings football game where they took on the Dallas Cowboys. This composition was a testament to his enduring connection with his home state and the local sports scene.

In a gesture of support for independent radio, Prince granted Minneapolis-area public radio station 89.3 The Current the honor of premiering his new song "Cause and Effect" the following month. This move showcased his ongoing commitment to championing unique and unconventional music platforms.

Prince's influence continued to reverberate worldwide, earning him a place in Time's prestigious annual list of the "100 Most Influential People in the World." This recognition underscored his enduring impact on the global music and cultural landscape.

On June 7, Prince celebrated his 52nd birthday by gifting the world a new single titled "Hot Summer," which debuted on Minneapolis radio station 89.3 The Current. The cover of the July 2010 issue of Ebony magazine featured Prince, honoring his illustrious career and lasting legacy. To cap it off, he received the esteemed Lifetime Achievement Award at the 2010 BET Awards, a testament to his remarkable contributions to the world of music.

Prince continued to showcase his innovative approach to music distribution by releasing his album "20Ten" in July 2010. This time, he chose an unconventional path by distributing it as a free covermount with various publications in the UK, Belgium, Germany, and France. In an era when digital downloads were gaining dominance, Prince opted to keep his music off digital download services, showing his unwavering commitment to unique and boundary-pushing methods of delivering his art.

On July 4, 2010, Prince embarked on his "20Ten Tour," thrilling audiences with his iconic performances. The tour was split into two legs, both held in Europe. The second leg featured a fresh lineup of talented musicians, including John Blackwell, Ida Kristine Nielsen, and Sheila E., creating a dynamic and captivating live experience for his fans.

Prince kept fans eagerly awaiting new music, debuting a snippet of his song "Rich Friends" from the album "20Ten Deluxe" on Europe 1 in October 2010. This preview offered a taste of his ever-evolving sound and songwriting.

As the year came to a close, Prince was far from slowing down. He embarked on the "Welcome 2 Tour" on December 15, 2010, treating audiences to a grand musical journey. His remarkable contributions to the music industry were further validated when he was inducted into the Grammy Hall of Fame on December 7, 2010, securing his place in the annals of music history.

Prince's presence continued to make a significant impact well into 2011. On February 12, he not only presented Barbra Streisand with an award but also demonstrated his philanthropic spirit by donating a generous $1.5 million to charitable causes, reflecting his commitment to making a positive difference in the world.

On the very same day, reports emerged that Prince had not granted authorization for the television show "Glee" to cover his hit song "Kiss." This decision to withhold his music from the show, despite the episode having already been filmed, underscored his unwavering stance on artistic control.

In a thrilling return to the stage, Prince headlined the Hop Farm Festival on July 3, 2011, marking his first live performance in the UK since 2007 and his inaugural appearance at a UK festival. Audiences were treated to an unforgettable show that rekindled the magic of his live performances.

While Prince had previously shunned the internet as a distribution platform for his music, a significant change occurred on November 24, 2011. He released a reworked version of the previously unreleased song "Extraloveable" on both iTunes and Spotify, embracing digital platforms as a means to share his music with a global audience.

Switzerland-based record label Purple Music played a role in expanding his musical horizons, releasing a CD single titled "Dance 4 Me" on December 12, 2011. This CD featured club remixes produced by Prince himself, adding a fresh dimension to his musical repertoire.

In January 2013, Prince continued to unveil new work, releasing a lyric video for the song "Screwdriver." The following April, he announced the "Live Out Loud Tour," with 3rdeyegirl as his backing band. The tour featured a special guest appearance by Bobby Z., the former drummer of Prince's Revolution, during the Minneapolis shows, further adding to the excitement.

Notably, in May 2013, Prince entered into a partnership with Kobalt Music to market and distribute his music, showcasing his forward-thinking approach to the ever-changing music industry landscape.

On August 14, 2013, he treated fans to another solo single titled "Breakfast Can Wait," featuring cover art that humorously portrayed comedian Dave Chappelle impersonating him, an homage to a memorable comedy sketch on Comedy Central's "Chappelle's Show."

February 2014 saw Prince performing a series of concerts in London with 3rdeyegirl as part of the "Hit and Run Tour." These intimate performances captivated audiences, reinforcing his status as a musical legend. He continued to surprise and delight fans with new music, releasing the single "The Breakdown" on April 18, 2014.

In a significant turn of events, Prince decided to rejoin forces with his former label, Warner Bros. Records, after an 18-year separation. This reunion was accompanied by the announcement that Prince would release a remastered deluxe edition of his iconic album "Purple Rain" in 2014, commemorating the 30th anniversary of the album's release. In exchange for this agreement, Warner granted Prince ownership of the master recordings of his works produced during his collaboration with the company, cementing his legacy as a pioneering artist.

In February 2014, Prince embarked on the 'Hit N Run Part One' tour, a venture marked by its unconventional and unpredictable nature. Fans and followers had to keep a close eye on Prince's Twitter feed for real-time updates on the whereabouts of his shows. Many of these concerts were announced on the day of the event, and some even featured two performances: one in the afternoon and another in the evening. The tour kicked off with 'Soundcheck' shows at Camden's Electric Ballroom in London and extended to other locations in the UK capital, including KoKo Club in Camden, Shepherd's Bush Empire, and various other intimate venues. After the London dates, Prince took the tour to other European cities.

In May 2014, Prince continued with his 'Hit N Run Part Two' shows, adopting a more conventional ticket purchasing approach and performing in larger music arenas. During this period, in the spring of 2014, he introduced NPG Publishing, a music company designed to oversee his own music and that of other artists without the constraints of traditional record companies, reflecting his commitment to artist autonomy.

In May 2015, following the death of Freddie Gray and the civil unrest that followed in Baltimore, Prince released the powerful song "Baltimore" as a tribute to Gray and in support of the protesters in the city. He went on to host a tribute concert at his Paisley Park estate, named "Dance Rally 4 Peace," where he encouraged attendees to wear the color gray as a mark of respect to Freddie

Gray. On May 10, Prince performed a special concert at the Royal Farms Arena in Baltimore, titled "Rally 4 Peace," which featured a guest appearance by Baltimore State's Attorney Marilyn Mosby and a set where Prince performed alone at a keyboard.

In the latter part of his career, Prince released two more albums. 'Hit n Run Phase One' became available on September 7, 2015, exclusively on the music streaming service Tidal, before seeing a CD and digital download release on September 14. His final album, 'Hit n Run Phase Two,' served as a continuation of this release strategy and was made accessible on Tidal for streaming and download on December 12, 2015.

In February 2016, Prince embarked on the Piano & A Microphone Tour, a unique showcase that stripped his performance down to the essentials: him and a custom piano on stage. He kicked things off with a series of warm-up shows at Paisley Park in late January 2016 before taking the tour to Melbourne, Australia, on February 16, 2016. The tour received widespread critical acclaim, and the Australian and New Zealand legs took place in small-capacity venues, including the iconic Sydney Opera House. Attendees at Hit n Run Phase Two shows received CDs of the album as part of their experience. Unfortunately, the tour was cut short in April 2016 due to health issues, marking the beginning of a challenging period for the iconic musician.

ILLNESS AND THE PASSING OF AN ICON

Tragically, Prince's final days were marked by health struggles that ultimately led to his untimely death. In the aftermath of his passing, a wave of grief and tribute from fans washed over the First Avenue nightclub, where they left flowers, purple balloons, and other keepsakes beneath Prince's star painted on the venue's front.

Prince's health issues became evident in April 2016. He consulted with Dr. Michael T. Schulenberg, a family medicine specialist in the Twin Cities. On April 7, Prince fell ill and postponed two shows from his Piano & a Microphone Tour at the Fox Theatre in Atlanta, with the venue attributing it to influenza. However, Prince rescheduled and performed what turned out to be his final show on April 14, despite his ongoing health struggles.

On his flight back to Minneapolis in the early morning of April 15, Prince became unresponsive, leading to an emergency landing of his private jet at Quad Cities International Airport in Moline, Illinois. He was subsequently hospitalized and administered naloxone, a medication used to counteract the effects of opioid overdoses. Once he regained consciousness, Prince left the hospital against medical advice. Official representatives stated that he had been suffering from influenza and dehydration for several weeks. Astonishingly, Prince was seen riding his bicycle the very next day in his hometown of Chanhassen and even went record shopping at the Electric Fetus in Minneapolis for Record Store Day. Later that evening, he made a brief appearance at an impromptu dance party held at his Paisley Park recording studio, reassuring those present that he was feeling well. On April 19, he attended a performance by singer Lizz Wright at the Dakota Jazz Club.

Seeking medical help for the music icon, Prince's representatives contacted Dr. Howard Kornfeld, a California specialist in addiction medicine and pain management, on April 20. Dr. Kornfeld arranged to meet with Prince on April 22 and contacted a local physician to perform a physical exam on April 21.

However, on the morning of April 21, the Carver County Sheriff's Office received a 911 call from Prince's Paisley Park home at 9:43 am. The caller initially reported an unconscious person at the residence but soon declared the individual as deceased, identifying the person as Prince. The caller was Dr. Kornfeld's son, who had arrived with buprenorphine that morning to help Prince with opioid addiction treatment.

Emergency responders discovered Prince unresponsive in an elevator, initiating CPR in an attempt to revive him. Tragically, he had already been dead for at least six hours, and their efforts proved unsuccessful. Prince was officially pronounced dead at 10:07 am, just 19 minutes after the arrival of emergency personnel. Authorities found no evidence of suicide or foul play.

On June 2, the Midwest Medical Examiner's Office in Anoka County released a press statement disclosing that Prince had tragically died of an accidental overdose of fentanyl, leaving a legacy that would forever reverberate in the world of music and entertainment. He passed away at the age of 57, leaving a void that would be deeply felt by his legions of fans and the music industry at large.

The fentanyl that led to Prince's tragic overdose was discovered in counterfeit pills designed to resemble a generic form of the painkiller hydrocodone/paracetamol. The investigation into how and from where Prince obtained the drug that ultimately caused his death has been a focal point for various law enforcement agencies. A sealed search warrant was issued for his estate, and another search warrant was unsealed for the local Walgreens pharmacy, shedding light on the efforts to uncover the source of the counterfeit medication.

However, on April 19, 2018, the Carver County Attorney's Office revealed that the multi-agency investigation into the circumstances of Prince's passing had concluded with no criminal charges filed. The details of how he came into possession of the counterfeit pills remained unanswered.

Following Prince's untimely demise, his remains were cremated after an autopsy performed by Dr. A. Quinn Strobl, who had trained under the tutelage of Janis Amatuzio. On April 26, 2016, Prince's sister and only full sibling, Tyka Nelson, initiated legal proceedings in Carver County to open a probate case, asserting that no will had been located. Prince, who was twice divorced and had no known surviving children, left behind a substantial estate comprising millions of dollars in cash, real estate, stocks, and vehicles. Under Minnesota law, the absence of a will entitled not only his full sister but also his five half-siblings to a share of the estate.

Within a mere three weeks of his passing, an astonishing 700 individuals claimed to be half-siblings or descendants, further complicating the matter. The Bremer Trust was granted temporary control over his estate, including permission to open his vault and collect a blood sample for DNA profiling from the coroner who conducted the autopsy.

To commemorate Prince's legacy, his ashes were placed in a specially designed 3D-printed urn, shaped like the iconic Paisley Park estate. This unique urn was put on public display in the atrium of the Paisley Park complex in October 2016.

As of April 2019, the courts had not recognized any additional claimants to the estate beyond Prince's full sister and five half-siblings. In August 2022, it was reported that the Prince estate had reached a settlement. Filings in the Minnesota First Judicial District dictated that the cash assets within Prince's estate be evenly divided between Prince Legacy LLC and Prince OAT Holdings LLC.

CHERISHED MEMORIES AND GLOBAL REACTIONS

The passing of Prince elicited an outpouring of grief and tributes from numerous musicians and cultural figures. President Obama joined in mourning his loss, and the United States Senate passed a resolution celebrating his contributions as a musician, composer, innovator, and cultural icon.

Cities throughout the United States paid their respects through tributes, vigils, and by illuminating buildings, bridges, and other structures in the color purple, a symbolic nod to Prince's unique persona.

In the immediate aftermath of the news of his death, "Prince" became the top trending term on Twitter within the first five hours. Facebook recorded a staggering 61 million interactions related to Prince.

MTV took the unprecedented step of interrupting its regular programming to broadcast a marathon of Prince's music videos and his iconic movie, Purple Rain. Movie theaters, including AMC Theatres and Carmike Cinemas, screened Purple Rain in select venues over the subsequent week.

Saturday Night Live, a show that had featured Prince on numerous occasions, dedicated an episode to him entitled "Goodnight, Sweet Prince." This special episode showcased some of his iconic performances from previous appearances on the show.

Nielsen Music reported an astounding 42,000 percent surge in the sales of his music. In the week following his passing, his catalog sold 4.41 million albums and songs, with the unprecedented occurrence of five of his albums simultaneously holding positions in the top ten of the Billboard 200 chart, setting a historic record.

At the 59th Grammy Awards, a heartfelt tribute to Prince was performed by Morris Day with the Time and Bruno Mars, further highlighting the enduring impact of this legendary artist on the world of music and culture.

Prince's influence and legacy continued to be celebrated and remembered in various ways following his passing:

- The May 2, 2016, cover of The New Yorker featured a striking illustration of purple rain, a direct reference to his iconic song.

- Vanity Fair/Condé Nast released a special edition commemorative magazine titled "The Genius of Prince" in June 2016. This magazine celebrated Prince's life and accomplishments with a collection of new photography and archive articles. The content included the original Vanity Fair article from November 1984, which was published in the wake of Prince's breakout success. The cover of the magazine featured a portrait of Prince by the renowned artist Andy Warhol, titled "Orange Prince" (1984).

- Broadway musicals also paid their respects to the star. During their curtain calls, the casts of "The Color Purple" and "Hamilton" honored Prince with renditions of "Purple Rain" and "Let's Go Crazy," respectively.

- In 2016, Minnesota representative Joe Atkins introduced a bill in the state legislature to commemorate Prince with a statue in the National Statuary Hall at the United States Capitol. This recognition aimed to honor Prince's contributions to music and the state of Minnesota. However, as of 2020, the bill had not progressed beyond the initial reading.

- Sinéad O'Connor, in her 2021 autobiography "Rememberings," shared details of unsettling experiences during her interactions with Prince. She described the fear among Prince's staff, attempted assault, and windows covered with tin foil. In interviews, she also mentioned that other women had shared similar experiences of feeling threatened in Prince's presence.

Prince's life and legacy continue to be remembered, both for his immense musical talents and for the complex and enigmatic personality he maintained throughout his career.

CONTINUING THE PURPLE REIGN

2016–2019

In the years following Prince's passing, a series of posthumous projects and developments unfolded. Notably, on August 21, 2016, Prince was posthumously inducted into the Rhythm and Blues Music Hall of Fame, recognizing his significant contributions to the genre.

Shortly after, the first album released after his death was a greatest hits compilation titled "4Ever," which saw the light of day on November 22, 2016. This compilation was notable for including one previously unreleased song, "Moonbeam Levels," recorded in 1982 during the "1999" album sessions.

Fast-forwarding to February 9, 2017, Prince's estate signed a distribution deal with Universal Music Group, encompassing the post-1995 recordings on his NPG Records label and unreleased tracks from his extensive music vault.

However, legal complications arose on June 27, 2017, as Comerica, acting on behalf of Prince's estate, requested that Carver County District Judge Kevin Eide cancel the estate's deal with Universal. The argument presented was that Universal's contract interfered with a prior agreement Prince had signed with Warner Music Group in 2014. After Universal's attorneys were allowed to examine the Warner contract, they offered to cancel their deal. On July 13, the court voided Universal's deal with Prince's estate. Nevertheless, Universal continued to handle Prince's songwriting credits and create merchandise.

Another notable occurrence took place on April 19 when an EP was announced, featuring six unreleased Prince recordings and titled "Deliverance." Initially, the release date was expected later in that week. However, the following day, Prince's estate was granted a temporary restraining order against George Ian Boxill, an engineer who co-produced the tracks and had possession of the master tapes. This legal action temporarily halted the release of the EP.

On June 23, a significant musical event unfolded with the re-release of Prince's iconic "Purple Rain" album. This marked the first Prince album to undergo a remastered and reissued treatment. The release came in two editions, the Deluxe and Deluxe Expanded versions. The Deluxe edition contained two discs. The first disc featured a remastered version of the original album, a meticulous process overseen by Prince himself back in 2015. The second disc was a treasure trove of previously unreleased songs, aptly titled "From the Vault & Previously Unreleased."

For those who craved even more, the Deluxe Expanded edition came with two additional discs. One of them comprised all the single edits, maxi-single edits, and B-sides from the Purple Rain era. The second bonus was a DVD that delighted fans with a concert from the Purple Rain Tour, filmed in Syracuse on March 30, 1985. This concert had previously been released on home video back in 1985.

The impact of this re-release was significant as the album made its return, debuting at No. 4 on the Billboard 200 chart, and claiming the top spot on both the Billboard R&B Albums and Vinyl Albums charts.

Fast forward to April 19, 2018, and a special treat was unveiled to Prince's fans. The original recording of "Nothing Compares 2 U" from 1984, which had never been released before, saw the light of day as a single through Warner Bros. in collaboration with Prince's estate. A music video was also crafted for the Prince version, featuring edited rehearsal footage from the Purple Rain tour, recorded during the summer of 1984. This exciting release came with the promise of a full-length album, scheduled for release on September 28, as announced by Troy Carter, an adviser for Prince's estate, in an interview with Variety.

Further developments took place in June when the Prince estate struck a distribution deal with Sony Music Entertainment. This deal encompassed the rights to all of Prince's studio albums, including unreleased music, remixes, live recordings, music videos, and B-sides from before 1995. Initially covering Prince's albums from 1995 to 2010, the distribution expanded further with a plan for

Prince's Warner Bros. albums from 1978 to 1996 to be distributed by Sony/Legacy Recordings in the United States, while Warner Music Group retained control of the international rights, starting in 2021.

In a series of posthumous events and releases, the legacy of Prince continued to resonate with fans and collectors alike. On July 11, 2018, Heritage Auctions revealed plans for an auction of Prince's personal items, to be held in Dallas, Texas on July 21, 2018. This eclectic collection included 27 items, such as Prince's bible, clothing he had worn on stage, and some of his personal documents.

Then, on August 17, NPG made a remarkable move, releasing all 23 post-Warner Bros. albums by Prince across various digital streaming platforms. Alongside this digital expansion, a new compilation album titled "Anthology: 1995-2010" was introduced, featuring 37 captivating tracks.

The enchanting journey into Prince's musical treasure trove didn't stop there. On September 21, music enthusiasts were treated to "Piano and a Microphone 1983," a collection released on CD, vinyl, and digital formats. This album was significant as it marked the first time the Prince estate offered material from the iconic musician's archive, known as the Vault.

The reissues of Prince's albums under the Sony/Legacy label commenced in February 2019, with the initial three releases being "Musicology," "3121," and "Planet Earth." These albums were made available on limited edition purple vinyl and standard CD formats. Additionally, the Prince Estate announced the reissues of "Rave Un2 the Joy Fantastic" and "Rave In2 the Joy Fantastic" on purple vinyl, and the release of "Ultimate Rave," a comprehensive 2 CD and 1 DVD set that included "Prince In Concert: Rave Un2 the Year 2000." In celebration of Record Store Day on April 13, the limited edition cassette "The Versace Experience - Prelude 2 Gold," originally issued in 1995 to attendees of Versace's 1995 Paris Fashion Week, was reissued.

June 7 brought a special release as Warner unveiled the new Prince album "Originals," exclusively on TIDAL. This unique collection featured Prince's original versions of 15 songs that he had previously offered to other artists. A broader release on CD and vinyl followed on June 20.

On September 13, "The Versace Experience" was reissued on purple vinyl and CD, accompanied by releases of "Chaos and Disorder" and "Emancipation." October 18 marked the release of a single containing Prince's acoustic demo of "I Feel for You," available in digital format as well as a limited edition 7" purple vinyl in honor of the 40th anniversary of the Prince album release.

The year continued to unravel more treasures. On November 27, "1999" was reissued in remastered, deluxe, and super deluxe editions. The super deluxe package included a staggering 35 previously unreleased songs and two thrilling live concerts.

Prince's posthumous journey was an enchanting odyssey for fans, revealing hidden gems from the musical genius's prolific career and unreleased material from his enigmatic Vault.

2020–2023

In recent years, the captivating and timeless music of Prince has seen a remarkable resurgence. The Estate of Prince Rogers Nelson has meticulously curated and presented some of his most iconic works in new and immersive ways.

A momentous event occurred on September 25, 2020, when Prince's landmark album "Sign o' the Times" received the royal treatment with the release of three distinct editions of "Sign o' the Times Super Deluxe." This event marked a significant milestone as it became the first Prince album to undergo a thorough remastering process. The Remastered edition, comprising the first two discs, offered fans a pristine version of the original album. It was a musical journey into Prince's world, overseen by the maestro himself in 2015, ensuring that the essence of the album remained intact. This remarkable remastering made the album sound as fresh as if it had been recorded yesterday.

For those seeking an even deeper dive into Prince's creative process, the Deluxe edition came to the rescue. This edition expanded upon the Remastered version by not only including the album but also a third disc that presented fans with all the single and maxi-single mixes, a true treasure trove for aficionados. Furthermore, the inclusion of the cherished B-sides added an extra layer of delight to the experience. These were the hidden gems that complemented the hit singles, enhancing the overall appeal of this Deluxe edition.

The most opulent offering was the Super Deluxe edition, a true feast for the senses. It featured six additional discs that allowed fans to immerse themselves in Prince's world like never before. Among these treasures were 45 previously unreleased studio tracks. These songs, some of which had been locked away in the vault for years, offered a glimpse into Prince's creative process and evolution as an artist. Hearing these tracks for the first time was akin to discovering a buried treasure chest of musical brilliance. It was a journey through the creative corridors of an enigmatic genius.

For those who crave the thrill of a live performance, the Super Deluxe edition did not disappoint. Two of the additional discs showcased the exhilarating live audio concert recordings of the Sign o' the Times Tour, which had taken place at the Galgenwaard stadium in Utrecht, The Netherlands. These audio recordings allowed fans to relive the electrifying atmosphere of a live Prince concert. It was a visceral experience, as if one were right there in the midst of a euphoric crowd, grooving to Prince's timeless hits.

The grand finale came in the form of a DVD, which held the live video concert recordings of the New Year's Eve show at Paisley Park. This iconic performance, previously available only through bootlegs, now graced the Super Deluxe edition. The visuals added a new dimension to the auditory journey, as fans could witness Prince's charisma and stage presence in all its glory. It was an unforgettable spectacle that captured the essence of Prince's live performances.

While the audio content was made accessible to fans in multiple formats, including vinyl in various editions, CD, and digital downloads on streaming platforms, the video content remained an exclusive feature of the physical DVD. It was a true collector's item, offering a unique and intimate look at one of Prince's legendary performances.

The impact of this release was immediate and profound. Pitchfork, the acclaimed music review platform, bestowed upon the Super Deluxe version a perfect 10 out of 10 rating and deemed it the Best New Reissue. Such accolades affirmed the significance of this release in celebrating the artistry of Prince.

Then, in April 2021, The Estate of Prince Rogers Nelson had more in store for fans. They announced the vinyl reissue of Prince's 1998 album "The Truth," timed to coincide with Record Store Day 2021. It was a delightful surprise for collectors and fans, allowing them to revisit this lesser-known gem in Prince's extensive discography.

In the days that followed, another revelation stirred excitement within the Prince community. The estate unveiled the upcoming release of an album titled "Welcome 2 America." This album was unique in that it contained never-before-heard material from Prince. It showcased his unparalleled talent and featured an ensemble of skilled musicians. Tal Wilkenfeld on bass, Chris Coleman on drums, Morris Hayes on keyboards, and vocals from New Power Generation singers Liv Warfield, Shelby J., and Elisa Fiorillo all contributed to the creation of this remarkable album.

"Welcome 2 America" was an auditory delight that allowed fans to witness Prince's genius in a fresh light. His lyrical prowess, musical dexterity, and unmistakable vocal range were on full display. It was an album that served as a testament to the enduring legacy of this musical icon. Released on July 30, 2021, it provided fans with another opportunity to experience the magic of Prince.

These recent years have seen the musical legacy of Prince continue to thrive. Thoughtful remasters, striking reissues, and previously unreleased gems have ensured that his work remains as vibrant and relevant as ever. Prince's influence on the world of music endures, and these releases are a testament to his enduring appeal and significance.

ARTISTRY

MUSICAL GENIUS AND ICONIC STYLE

Prince's impact on the music industry and his artistic legacy are nothing short of extraordinary. He is widely acclaimed as one of the greatest musicians of his generation, leaving an indelible mark on the world of music and beyond. Rolling Stone, a prestigious authority on music, recognized Prince's significance by ranking him at No. 27 on their list of the 100 Greatest Artists of the rock & roll era, highlighting his enduring influence. According to Acclaimed Music, a prominent music rating source, Prince holds the esteemed title of the 9th most celebrated artist in the history of popular music.

Prince's artistic brilliance did not go unnoticed during his lifetime. In 2010, VH1 crowned him as the 7th greatest artist of all time, a testament to his timeless appeal. His vocal prowess was equally legendary, and in 2023, Rolling Stone acknowledged this by placing Prince at an impressive No. 16 on their list of the 200 Greatest Singers of All Time.

The recognition of Prince's iconic albums and songs further solidifies his status in music history. In 2003, Rolling Stone featured several of his albums on their list of the 500 Greatest Albums of All Time, with "Purple Rain" securing the 72nd spot, "Sign o' the Times" at No. 93, "1999" taking the 163rd place, and "Dirty Mind" landing at No. 204. In addition, Rolling Stone's list of the 500 Greatest Songs of All Time in 2004 celebrated his tracks, including "When Doves Cry" at No. 52, "Little Red Corvette" ranking 108th, "Purple Rain" at a commendable No. 143, "1999" standing proudly at No. 212, "Sign o' the Times" making its mark at No. 299, and "Kiss" captivating audiences at No. 461.

Prince's music transcended boundaries and defied categorization. The Los Angeles Times aptly referred to him as "our first post-everything pop star," emphasizing his ability to challenge conventional labels of race, genre, and commercial appeal. Jon Pareles of The New York Times recognized him as a "master architect of funk, rock, R&B, and pop," highlighting his unique ability to defy traditional genres. Geoffrey Himes acknowledged Prince's role as a leading artist in the realm of "progressive soul," a term he believed might be somewhat limiting but indicative of Prince's innovative musical landscape.

Prince's versatility in music is an overarching theme that captivated audiences throughout his career. He seamlessly navigated between funk, rock, R&B, and pop, showcasing a musical prowess that defied easy classification. Simon Reynolds described him as a "pop polymath" who effortlessly incorporated funkadelia, acid rock, deep soul, and schmaltz within the same song. AllMusic recognized Prince's remarkable stylistic evolution and genre diversity with each album, emphasizing his unique ability to merge diverse styles into a cohesive whole.

The era of the album in music was dominated by Prince's contributions, earning him a place in the pantheon of artists who defined this period. His impact extended far beyond his genre-bending music, making him an enduring icon in the music world and a true artist of unparalleled influence.

Prince was more than just a musician; he was an enigmatic performer known for his extravagant style and captivating showmanship. His flamboyance on stage became one of his defining traits, leaving audiences in awe. He was celebrated as a sex symbol, a testament to his androgynous and gender-fluid allure. Prince defied conventional gender norms and played with gender signifiers, pushing the boundaries of expression. His fashion sense was as audacious and idiosyncratic as his music, often featuring his iconic color, purple, enchanting makeup, and frilled garments. His androgynous look drew comparisons to rock 'n' roll pioneers like Little Richard and the legendary David Bowie.

Prince's bold fashion choices weren't just for show; they held deeper significance. His '80s gender-defying style resonates even more in our current trans-aware era, while simultaneously harking back to the roots of rock 'n' roll with its blend of racial and sexual influences. Throughout his career, Prince championed strong female presence in his bands and offered unwavering support for women in the music industry. He collaborated with an astounding array of female stars, promising a world where gender lines blurred and everyone was free to express themselves. On and off the stage, Prince was never shy to embrace high-heeled shoes and boots.

His influence extended far beyond his music, inspiring a multitude of artists from various genres. The likes of Beyoncé, Justin Timberlake, Bruno Mars, Rihanna, and Alicia Keys all found inspiration in Prince's innovative artistry. His impact even reached into the realms of rock, with artists like Lenny Kravitz and Marilyn Manson crediting him as a driving force in their careers. Prince's influence was felt in contemporary R&B and pop with artists such as The Weeknd, Lady Gaga, and Lorde, as well as the realms of hip-hop, where André 3000 and Usher found inspiration in his work. This enduring influence is a testament to Prince's timeless and boundary-breaking artistry.

Bono of U2, one of the most iconic rock bands of the 20th century, regarded Prince as one of his "favorite composers of the twentieth century," acknowledging the depth and brilliance of his musical creations. In a heartfelt expression of admiration, Beyoncé referred to Prince as her mentor, praising his courage in fighting for his creative freedom through words and music.

In August 2017, Prince's legacy was immortalized through Pantone Inc., who introduced a new shade of purple in his honor, known as Love Symbol #2. This color, forever linked to Prince, serves as a vivid symbol of his enduring impact on the world of music and art.

INFLUENCES AND ARTISTIC EXPERTISE

Prince's music was a brilliant amalgamation of diverse influences that showcased his unparalleled musicianship. His unique sound was an eclectic blend, drawing inspiration from a vast array of musical legends. Some of the notable figures who left their imprint on Prince's musical journey include:

- **Ike Turner:** The influential Ike Turner's contributions to rock and R&B had a significant impact on Prince's music.

- **James Brown:** Known as the "Godfather of Soul," James Brown's funk and soul elements heavily influenced Prince's sound.

- **George Clinton:** The mastermind behind P-Funk, George Clinton's innovative funk music played a crucial role in shaping Prince's musical style.

- **Joni Mitchell:** The iconic folk singer and songwriter Joni Mitchell inspired Prince with her poetic and introspective songwriting.

- **Duke Ellington:** The legendary jazz artist Duke Ellington's rich and complex arrangements left a mark on Prince's approach to music.

- **Jimi Hendrix:** The groundbreaking guitar virtuoso Jimi Hendrix was a significant influence on Prince's guitar skills and stage presence.

- **The Beatles:** The Fab Four, the Beatles, contributed to Prince's diverse musical palette with their innovative songwriting and experimentation.

- **Chuck Berry:** The rock and roll pioneer Chuck Berry's signature guitar riffs and energetic performances resonated with Prince's music.

- **David Bowie:** The enigmatic David Bowie's artistic creativity and genre-blurring style had a profound impact on Prince.

- **Earth, Wind & Fire:** The elements of funk and soul from Earth, Wind & Fire played a role in shaping Prince's distinctive sound.

- **Mick Jagger:** The frontman of the Rolling Stones, Mick Jagger, influenced Prince's stage presence and showmanship.

- **Rick James:** Known for his funk and soul music, Rick James' style and energy were an inspiration to Prince.

- **Jerry Lee Lewis:** The rock and roll pioneer Jerry Lee Lewis's piano skills contributed to the rich tapestry of Prince's music.

- **Little Richard:** Little Richard's groundbreaking contributions to rock and roll left an indelible mark on Prince's musical journey.

- **Curtis Mayfield:** Curtis Mayfield's soulful and socially conscious music resonated with Prince's approach to songwriting.

- **Elvis Presley:** The King of Rock and Roll, Elvis Presley, influenced Prince's exploration of different musical styles.

- **Todd Rundgren:** Todd Rundgren's progressive and experimental music inspired Prince's approach to music production.

- **Carlos Santana:** The legendary guitarist Carlos Santana had an impact on Prince's guitar techniques and musical diversity.

- **Sly Stone:** Sly Stone's pioneering funk music influenced Prince's sound and funkadelic elements.

- **Jackie Wilson:** Jackie Wilson's soulful performances and vocal prowess were sources of inspiration for Prince.

- **Stevie Wonder:** The musical genius Stevie Wonder's melodic and harmonic innovations influenced Prince's songwriting and music.

Prince's ability to synthesize these diverse influences and create a sound uniquely his own set him apart as a musical icon. He was often compared to jazz legend Miles Davis, acknowledging the artistic changes throughout his career. In fact, Miles Davis once described Prince as an otherworldly blend of musical giants like James Brown, Jimi Hendrix, Marvin Gaye, Sly Stone, Little Richard, Duke Ellington, and Charlie Chaplin. Their collaborative performance at Paisley Park is remembered as the pinnacle of their artistic partnership, capturing the essence of their shared musical genius.

Prince was more than just a musical virtuoso; he was hailed as "rock's greatest ever natural talent" by journalist Nik Cohn. His musical prowess extended across multiple dimensions:

Vocal Mastery

Prince was a natural tenor but possessed a remarkable vocal range that spanned from falsetto to baritone. He effortlessly executed rapid shifts between registers, showcasing the full extent of his vocal artistry.

Multi-Instrumental Genius

Beyond his vocal talents, Prince's true virtuosity shone as a multi-instrumentalist. He demonstrated mastery over various musical instruments, including guitar, drums, percussion, bass, keyboards, and synthesizers. On his initial five albums, he played nearly every instrument, an astounding feat that showcased his versatility. His debut album alone featured him playing 27 different instruments.

Innovative Technophile

Prince was a pioneer in embracing technology to enhance his music. He was an early adopter of drum machines, such as the Linn LM-1, which became integral to his sound in the early '80s. He also harnessed a wide array of studio effects to shape his music. His use of new-generation synthesizer sounds laid the foundation for the evolution of post-'70s funk music.

Prolific Songwriting

Prince's prolific songwriting abilities extended beyond his own catalog. He penned songs for other artists, leaving an indelible mark on the music industry. Some of his compositions, like "Manic Monday" performed by The Bangles, "I Feel For You" covered by Chaka Khan, and "Nothing

Compares 2 U" famously interpreted by Sinéad O'Connor, became hit songs in their own right.

Collaborative Songwriting

Prince was known for collaborating with other artists. He co-wrote "Love... Thy Will Be Done" with singer Martika and gifted Celine Dion with a song, "With This Tear," written specifically for her. He also wrote "U" for Paula Abdul, further demonstrating his versatility and collaborative spirit.

Prince's diverse talents transcended traditional boundaries, and his innovative spirit continues to influence and inspire musicians across generations.

ICONIC GUITARS

Prince was not only a master of music but also had a distinct flair for iconic guitars, each uniquely associated with his legendary career. Here are some of his signature and custom guitars:

HS Anderson/Hohner Madcat Telecaster Copy (197?)

One of Prince's early iconic guitars, the HS Anderson Madcat Telecaster copy, was a testament to his unique style.

Cloud Guitar White (1983)

The Cloud Guitar in white was an iconic symbol of Prince's persona. Its distinctive design captured his imaginative and artistic spirit.

Cloud Guitar Gold (1983)

Another variation of the Cloud Guitar, this time in gold, showcased Prince's penchant for blending style and substance.

Model C (19??)

The Model C is a mysterious entry in Prince's collection, adding an air of intrigue to his guitar choices.

Cloud Guitar Yellow (1989)

The Cloud Guitar in yellow demonstrated Prince's commitment to making a bold statement through his choice of instruments.

Cloud Guitar Blue (19??)

Prince's blue Cloud Guitar added yet another layer to the enigmatic and artistic aura he exuded.

Gold Fender Stratocaster (????)

While details remain scarce, the Gold Fender Stratocaster was surely another one of Prince's treasures.

Prince Symbol Purple (19??)

Symbolic of Prince's unapologetic uniqueness, the purple Prince Symbol guitar became an extension of his persona.

Prince Symbol Gold (19??)

A gold variation of his iconic Symbol guitar, further solidifying the legendary status of this instrument.

G1 Purple Special (2007)

The G1 Purple Special was a testament to Prince's love for his signature color, purple.

Gus G3 Prince Bass (2016)

A more recent addition, the Gus G3 Prince Bass, represented his enduring passion for creating music.

Each of these guitars played a role in shaping the iconic sounds of Prince's music, making them not just instruments but essential elements of his artistry.

EQUIPMENT

Prince's mastery as a guitarist extended to his dazzling collection of custom guitars, boasting a total of 121 remarkable instruments. Among his prized guitars, the Cloud Guitars stand out as iconic creations, released in distinct colors, including white, yellow, and purple. Notably, the white Cloud Guitar took the spotlight in the "Purple Rain" film and the "Raspberry Beret" music video, adding a touch of visual artistry to his performances.

Equally striking were The Love Symbol guitars, meticulously designed in resplendent gold and regal purple, embodying the essence of his musical royalty. Throughout his illustrious career, the H.S. Anderson Madcat guitar, a Telecaster copy crafted by Hohner, took center stage as his primary musical companion. Its journey encompassed multiple iterations, some graciously donated for charitable purposes, while others were regrettably stolen.

In his later years, another significant addition to his collection was the Vox HDC-77, introduced to him by fellow musician Ida Kristine Nielsen, a member of 3rdeyegirl. It came in two captivating versions, one in Black Burst and the other in White Ivory, showcasing his ongoing quest for innovative soundscapes.

Two guitars of particular note within his extensive collection were the G1 Purple Special, which resonated with his beloved color, and the black-and-gold Gus G3 Prince bass. These guitars held special significance, as they became the final additions to his impressive array of musical instruments, sealing his legacy as a virtuoso who pushed the boundaries of music and style.

LEGAL BATTLES

CREATIVE PSEUDONYMS

In 1993, a significant legal dispute arose between Prince and Warner Bros. concerning the release of his album "The Gold Experience." This legal battle centered on the issues of artistic and financial control of Prince's musical creations. In a powerful and visually striking statement, Prince appeared in public with the word "slave" boldly written on his cheek. This provocative action was a manifestation of his frustration with the situation, as he sought to free himself from the constraints of his contract with Warner Bros.

As a dramatic step towards asserting his independence, Prince decided to change his name to an unpronounceable symbol. This symbol represented his emancipation from the contract and conveyed his sentiment that his very name had become a commodity owned by the company.

Prince also had a penchant for using pseudonyms throughout his career. He employed these aliases to separate his identity from the music he had composed, produced, or recorded. It was his way of expressing that the act of sharing his creative ideas reinforced his ownership and creative achievement. Among the pseudonyms he adopted at various points were "Jamie Starr" and "The Starr Company," which he used for songs he wrote for the Time and numerous other artists from 1981 to 1984. He also used "Joey Coco" for a range of unreleased Prince tracks in the late 1980s and for songs penned for artists like Sheena Easton and Kenny Rogers. Additionally, he adopted the name "Alexander Nevermind" when he wrote the song "Sugar Walls" for Sheena Easton in 1984, and the simple moniker "Christopher" was employed for his songwriting credit on "Manic Monday" for the Bangles in 1986.

COPYRIGHT BATTLES

In 2007, Prince found himself embroiled in legal battles over copyright issues. The iconic musician took a stand against YouTube and eBay, alleging that they had been hosting his copyrighted material without proper authorization. To tackle this challenge, he enlisted the services of Web Sheriff, an international Internet-policing company.

During the same year, a woman named Stephanie Lenz filed a lawsuit against Universal Music Publishing Group. Her claim was that the music publisher had misused copyright laws by having her homemade video removed from YouTube. This video featured the faint background presence of Prince's song "Let's Go Crazy."

In response to the perceived crackdown on the use of Prince-related content, a group of fan sites united to create "Prince Fans United." Their primary objective was to counteract legal requests initiated by Prince that, according to the fans, seemed to limit the use of various Prince-related materials, such as photographs, images, lyrics, album covers, and anything associated with his likeness. In Prince's legal team's view, such usage amounted to copyright infringement, but the Prince Fans United group insisted that these legal actions were actually attempts to stifle any critical commentary or discussion about Prince. Interestingly, AEG, the promoter for Prince, argued that the only contentious items on the three fan sites were live photos taken during Prince's 21-night residency at the O2 Arena in London earlier that year.

As a reaction to this fan initiative, on November 8, Prince Fans United received a song titled "PFUnk." This song was a sort of unofficial response to their movement and initially premiered on the PFU main site. It was later retitled "F.U.N.K." and intriguingly was not available for purchase on the iTunes Store.

These legal actions and their ensuing consequences didn't conclude here. On November 14, a satirical website, b3ta.com, pulled down its "image challenge of the week" dedicated to Prince due to legal threats from the artist. Prince cited violations of the Digital Millennium Copyright Act (DMCA) as the reason behind this action.

These incidents shed light on Prince's determination to protect his intellectual property and his engagement in legal battles to ensure his music was used in compliance with copyright laws.

It also highlights the challenges posed by the changing landscape of online content sharing and copyright enforcement during that time.

At the 2008 Coachella Valley Music and Arts Festival, often referred to as Coachella Festival, Prince took the stage and delivered a memorable performance, including a cover of Radiohead's "Creep." Yet, his actions following this event garnered significant attention. Almost immediately, he insisted that footage of the performance, which fans had recorded, be removed from YouTube and other platforms. This move raised eyebrows, especially considering that Radiohead had specifically requested that the video remain accessible online. Fortunately, a few days later, YouTube reinstated the videos, following Radiohead's statement that "It's our song, let people hear it." In 2009, Prince uploaded the video of his Coachella performance on his official website.

In 2010, Prince made a bold declaration, stating, "the internet is completely over." He would go on to explain this statement in 2015, expressing his belief that "the internet was over for anyone who wants to get paid." According to him, it was challenging for musicians to amass wealth through digital sales in that evolving landscape.

However, Prince's relationship with the online world was not without controversy. In 2013, the Electronic Frontier Foundation presented Prince with the inaugural "Raspberry Beret Lifetime Aggrievement Award." This recognition was based on their assessment that Prince had abused the DMCA takedown process, raising concerns about the way he had handled digital rights and copyright issues.

In January 2014, Prince initiated legal action titled "Prince v. Chodera" against 22 online users, accusing them of direct copyright infringement, unauthorized fixation, contributory copyright infringement, and bootlegging. Notably, some of the users were fans who had shared links to bootlegged versions of Prince's concerts through social media platforms such as Facebook. Surprisingly, Prince dismissed the entire case without prejudice later in the same month.

Prince's approach to his music also extended to parodies. Notably, he was one of the few musicians to deny "Weird Al" Yankovic permission to parody his songs. It's worth noting that Yankovic doesn't require legal permission to parody songs, but he typically seeks artists' approval as a professional courtesy. Prince's rejection of these requests was distinctive in that he offered no explanation beyond a simple, unequivocal "no."

PRIVATE LIFE

Prince's personal life was marked by his romantic involvement with numerous women throughout his career, leaving a trail of well-known relationships with celebrities such as Kim Basinger, Madonna, Vanity, Jill Jones, Sheila E., Carmen Electra, Susannah Melvoin, and Sherilyn Fenn. Susannah Melvoin, in particular, shared a unique connection with Prince, as they lived together with Lisa Coleman, forming a close-knit family. She reflected on that time, noting how they had the privilege of having Prince as an integral part of their lives.

In 1990, Prince encountered 16-year-old dancer Mayte García outside his tour bus and prophesied her as his "future wife" while introducing her to fellow bandmate Rosie Gaines. García's journey with Prince began when she joined his team as a backup singer and dancer after her high school graduation. The couple's romantic journey led them to marriage on February 14, 1996, when Prince was 37, and García was 22. However, their happiness was marred by tragedy when their son, Amiir, born on October 16, 1996, succumbed to Pfeiffer syndrome just a week after birth. The details of their child's name, birth, and the cause of death were shrouded in secrecy due to Prince's strong commitment to privacy. The weight of this loss and García's subsequent miscarriage took a toll on their marriage, leading to their divorce in 2000.

Subsequently, Prince tied the knot with Manuela Testolini, a Canadian businesswoman of Italian and Egyptian descent, in an intimate ceremony in 2001. The couple divided their time between various locations, including Toronto. Unfortunately, their marriage faced its challenges, and they separated in 2005, finalizing their divorce in May 2006.

Beyond his music, Prince was known for his dedication to animal rights and an evolving dietary regimen. He began as a vegan and transitioned to a vegetarian diet at various points in his life. His journey towards a plant-based diet started around 1987 when he ceased consuming red meat. Prince also followed a pescetarian diet during the 2000s. At Paisley Park, his private residence and production complex, he imposed dietary preferences on guests and staff, requiring them to follow a vegetarian or pescetarian diet while on the premises. This commitment to a meatless environment at Paisley Park endures as part of Prince's legacy. Additionally, Prince's concern for animal welfare was evident in the liner notes of his album "Rave Un2 the Joy Fantastic," where he spoke out against the cruelty associated with wool production.

Mayte García shed light on Prince's spiritual beliefs, describing him as a perpetual seeker of spiritual truths. He exhibited a fascination with a wide spectrum of beliefs, including the integration of zodiac signs, the third eye, and reincarnation into his Christian faith. The foundation of his spirituality was influenced by the Baptist faith of his mother and the Seventh-day Adventist beliefs of his father.

In 2001, Prince embarked on a profound spiritual journey, which led him to become a Jehovah's Witness. His path to this faith was the culmination of a two-year discussion with bassist Larry Graham, who not only became his mentor but also a cherished friend during this period. Prince regarded this transition not as a conversion but as a "realization." To illustrate his sentiment, he drew a parallel between his transformation and the relationship between Morpheus and Neo in the movie "The Matrix" (1999). He actively participated in meetings at a local Kingdom Hall and even engaged in door-to-door discussions to share his newfound faith with others.

During this phase of his life, Prince grappled with the need for double hip replacement surgery, a condition he had faced since 2005. At the time, tabloids disseminated an unverified rumor suggesting that his religious beliefs, which included a refusal to accept blood transfusions, were a barrier to undergoing the operation. Larry Graham, however, countered these claims, affirming that medical technology offered alternatives to blood transfusions. Jimmy Jam, a longtime collaborator, remarked on Prince's ordeal, acknowledging the immense pain he must have endured due to his hip issues.

Prince's philanthropic and charitable endeavors often flew under the radar during his lifetime. It was only after his passing that the extent of his generosity came to light. In 2001, he anonymously donated $12,000 to the Louisville Free Public Library system to prevent the closure of the historic Western Branch Library, the nation's first full-service library for African-Americans. During the same period, Prince anonymously covered the medical expenses of drummer Clyde Stubblefield, who was undergoing cancer treatment. In 2015, he initiated and funded the YesWeCode program, supporting various hackathons and even performing at some events. Prince also played a crucial role in financing the Green for All initiative.

In a late March 2016 performance, Prince confided to his audience that he was in the process of writing a memoir titled "The Beautiful Ones." Despite his untimely demise, his co-writer, Dan Piepenbring, continued working on the memoir. The book, titled "The Beautiful Ones," was eventually published in October 2019, providing readers with a deeper glimpse into the enigmatic artist's life.

ACHIEVEMENTS

Prince's impact on the music industry is nothing short of monumental, with record sales surpassing 150 million worldwide. This remarkable achievement places him among the elite group of best-selling music artists in history. His influence and talent were widely recognized, earning him a place in the Rock and Roll Hall of Fame in 2004, the UK Music Hall of Fame in 2006, and the Rhythm and Blues Music Hall of Fame in 2016.

In 2016, posthumous recognition came in the form of a Doctor of Humane Letters awarded by the University of Minnesota, celebrating his contributions to both music and society. Additionally, Prince was inducted into the Black Music & Entertainment Walk of Fame in 2022, commemorating his lasting legacy.

The music legend's virtuosity on the guitar was acknowledged by Rolling Stone, which named him the 14th greatest guitarist of all time in 2023. Prince's eclectic and innovative style earned him an array of prestigious awards, including seven Grammy Awards, seven Brit Awards, six American Music Awards, four MTV Video Music Awards, an Academy Award for Best Original Song Score for the film "Purple Rain," and a Golden Globe Award. Notably, two of his albums, "Purple Rain" and "Sign o' the Times," received Grammy Award nominations for Album of the Year.

His contributions to music have left an indelible mark, with albums like "1999," "Purple Rain," and "Sign o' the Times" being inducted into the Grammy Hall of Fame. At the 28th Grammy Awards, Prince was honored with the President's Merit Award, recognizing his extraordinary influence on the music industry. Furthermore, he received accolades at the American Music Awards, including the American Music Award for Achievement and the American Music Award of Merit in 1990 and 1995, respectively.

In 2013, Prince was celebrated with the Billboard Icon Award at the Billboard Music Awards, underscoring his enduring significance in the world of music. His cultural impact extended beyond the realm of music, with the 1984 film "Purple Rain" earning a place in the Library of Congress's National Film Registry in 2019 due to its cultural, historical, and aesthetic significance.

In his hometown of Minneapolis, Prince was honored with a star on the outside mural of the legendary First Avenue nightclub, a prestigious recognition reserved for performers who have played sold-out shows or made a significant cultural contribution to the venue. This star is not just a symbol of his success but a testament to his profound impact on the local music scene. The star, originally silver like others on the mural, was transformed into a golden tribute in May 2016, following Prince's untimely passing. The artist behind this transformation was revealed to be Peyton Russell, a graphic designer and graffiti artist who had worked for Prince at his club Glam Slam in the 1990s. His act of paying homage to Prince was a heartfelt gesture, etching the artist's legacy even more deeply into the culture of Minneapolis.

HONORED LEGACY

On May 9, 2023, a momentous tribute to the legendary musician took place in Minnesota. Governor Tim Walz made history by signing a bill into law that officially dedicated a portion of Minnesota State Highway 5, spanning from Chanhassen to Eden Prairie, as the "Prince Rogers Nelson Memorial Highway." This symbolic stretch of road passes right by Paisley Park, the hallowed ground where Prince's musical genius thrived.

In a fitting nod to the artist's iconic use of the color purple, the road signs for this memorial highway were uniquely designated to be purple, setting them apart from the customary brown signage seen on highways. This special exception was granted by the Minnesota Department of Transportation, as the color purple is traditionally reserved for toll roads, making it a distinctive and poignant tribute to the beloved Prince.

EPILOGUE

In the annals of music history, Prince stands as a truly incomparable artist, a creative force that defied convention and continually pushed the boundaries of what music could be. His extraordinary career spanned decades, leaving an indelible mark on the industry and a lasting legacy of innovation, audacity, and unwavering artistry.

Prince was a virtuoso, a master of multiple instruments, and a vocal powerhouse with a range that traversed from falsetto to baritone. His performances were electrifying, characterized by his flamboyant style, magnetic stage presence, and a unique blend of rock, funk, R&B, and pop. His music, marked by its sensual lyrics and provocative themes, was as transformative as the artist himself, provoking thought and sparking change in society's perception of gender, sexuality, and race.

Throughout his career, Prince maintained an air of mystery, often hiding behind pseudonyms and challenging conventional expectations. His independence and refusal to conform to industry norms illustrated his relentless pursuit of creative freedom. His journey took him from a legal battle with Warner Bros. Records, which led to his iconic name change to an unpronounceable symbol, to his later embrace of technology in music production, pioneering the use of drum machines and innovative studio effects.

Prince was a spiritual seeker, embarking on a personal journey that led him to embrace the faith of Jehovah's Witnesses, yet he retained his fascination with a myriad of spiritual concepts and beliefs. His commitment to these convictions was as unwavering as his commitment to his art.

His influence extended far beyond the stage. He was a dedicated activist, philanthropist, and humanitarian, championing various causes and anonymously supporting those in need. He made significant contributions to social and technological advancements, including his support for YesWeCode, which encouraged diversity in the technology industry.

In the end, Prince's story is one of musical genius, a relentless pursuit of creative freedom, and a profound impact on the world. He may have left this earthly realm in 2016, but his music, spirit, and unceasing innovation remain alive, inspiring new generations of artists to explore their own creative boundaries. Prince's enigmatic journey will continue to captivate and inspire for generations to come, reminding us that true artistry knows no bounds and that the artist himself was, and always will be, a symbol of the extraordinary.

Made in the USA
Las Vegas, NV
01 April 2024

88063496R00100